Parrot

Animal

Series editor: Jonathan Burt

Already published

Crow
Boria Sax

Ant
Charlotte Sleigh

Tortoise
Peter Young

Cockroach
Marion Copeland

Dog
Susan McHugh

Oyster
Rebecca Stott

Bear
Robert E. Bieder

Rat
Jonathan Burt

Snake
Drake Stutesman

Falcon
Helen Macdonald

Bee
Claire Preston

Forthcoming

Whale
Joe Roman

Hare
Simon Carnell

Moose
Kevin Jackson

Fly
Steven Connor

Tiger
Susie Green

Fox
Martin Wallen

Crocodile
Richard Freeman

Spider
Katja and Sergiusz Michalski

Duck
Victoria de Rijke

Salmon
Peter Coates

Wolf
Garry Marvin

Parrot

Paul Carter

REAKTION BOOKS

Published by
REAKTION BOOKS LTD
33 Great Sutton Street
London EC1V ODX

www.reaktionbooks.co.uk

First published 2006
Copyright © Paul Carter 2006

Printed in China

British Library Cataloguing in Publication Data
Carter, Paul, 1951–
    Parrot. – (Animal)
    1. Parrots 2. Animals and civilization
    I. Title
    595.7'1

ISBN 1 86189 237 3

Contents

Preface: Cage, Net, Web

Say 'parrot', and most people think they know what you mean. Writing this book, I found saying parrot was a great conversation opener. It sounds like a joke, it breaks the ice, and before you know where you are, everyone has a parrot story to tell. One anecdote leads to another; there are giggles and guffaws; it's like a party of galahs. But go a little deeper and ask your friends what *image* of parrots they have, and it's a different matter. Is it a blue and yellow macaw that comes to mind? Or a cockatoo? Or a budgerigar? A green parrot or a grey one? Or does some kind of overall parrot flash up in the mind's eye when we start telling stories about these extraordinary creatures that talk like us?

The astonishing truth is that no clear picture of parrot informs our chatter. Beyond the barest gestalt of beak and claws, and a general avian character, the idea of parrot circulates in our culture without any reference to birds living in the wild. In Europe and America this might be explained by the absence of naturally occurring parrots to populate our earliest memories, but in Australia it's the same. Australia's embarrassment of psittacine riches does not mean that any two people are talking about the same thing. It seems, in fact, that parrot does not refer to a winged emanation *out there*. It names a mental creature bred inside the cage of language; and we keep it there, talking to it, repeating what it says back to us, not because of the beauty of its plumes, but because it gives us a reason to talk. Parrot signifies the desire to communicate. This is why, inside the cage of language, it circulates so freely.

Yet *Parrot* is also about something else. *Outside* language, whether in their rapidly disappearing jungles or in the eugenicist groves of aviculture – parrots are being hunted and bred to death. Western technocratic capitalism is an investment in global communication. The electronic net in which it seeks to capture every exchange accelerates the consumption of the earth's spiritual and material resources. Our culture – the one without boundaries in which a book like *Parrot* is read – is systematically pursuing the extinction of its own totem. This is the particular poignancy of attempts to conserve parrot populations and habitats: our fate as a culture capable of talking its way out of trouble is directly related to our ability to imagine parrot differently.

Parrots do not imitate other birds in the wild, and they only talk in captivity. These facts suggest to me that parrot's inside history – the way it circulates in the collective imagination – and outside history – measured in an accelerating rate of biological destruction – are interrelated. Because we are captives of our own representations we cannot imagine communicating differently. We persist in thinking that parrots merely mimic us, when their mimicry is a way of telling us that we are mimics. But what parrots are telling us will emerge only when we listen to them differently. When communication is imagined as a net, not a cage, and the net is conceived as an architecture organizing free relations, an open web, not a more powerful technique of enslavement – only then will our symbolic and material economies be harmonized.

Parrot is parasitic on previous studies but, as an essay in the communication of parrot, it differs. Natural histories of parrots

assume the existence of objectively knowable parrots out there. They provide as comprehensive a representation of these as possible. Cultural histories likewise assume parrot representations are empirically based. They narrate the degree of misrepresentation parrots suffer in different cultures as they morph into collective symbols. But *Parrot* is different: tracking the ramifying web of parrot associations, as parrot circulates in the collective imaginary, it begins and ends in a lesson parrots teach us – repetitions are without originals, and mimics are telling us this. In a way, without parrots we cannot be human. If nothing else, I hope *Parrot* communicates this.

Shouldering a burden or 'pieces-of-eight'? Rich, reputedly the world's richest parrot.

Introduction: Communicating Parrots

Parrothood is not easy to define.

Hillel Schwartz[1]

Parrothood is not easy to *hear* either. Repeatedly, I was heard to say I was writing a book about *parents, Paris, pirates,* even *parody,* but never or rarely a book about parrots. Such mishearings were partly a symptom of surprise: I had said the wrong thing in the wrong place (rather like parrots do). Parrot fanciers, aviculturalists, men with guns and nets, animal psychologists and naturalists are qualified to cut a swathe through the sprawling forest of parrot lore – but yours truly is none of these. If, as Jean Cocteau says, everyone carries a parrot on their shoulder, then it's no less the case that almost everyone has a budgie in their background. Our neighbour's sky blues trustingly perched on my head (a no-no in well-bred avicultural circles) and politely shat on the evening newspaper laid out for them – my first exposure to the return of the repressed. In Australia, I found by sidelong enquiry (another parrot trait I picked up) that a sharp nip from a cockatoo was part of every young woman's growing up. But such casual encounters, while they must signify something, hardly suggest that the great parrot god – on the authority of Wallace Stevens ('Above the forest of parrakeets,/ A parrakeet of parrakeets prevails.')[2] – had uniquely passed over my house, marking me as a future parrot-man.

My interest in parrots started elsewhere, as parrots swam into my ken as types of the Other (geographically and socially)

Lip-nipping: in Jeff Carter's photograph love comes with strings attached – notice the cage in the background.

par excellence. An early obsession with birds had taken me to India and Mexico, but parrots hardly featured in those travels. Perhaps a clue to their invisibility is contained in nineteenth-century parrot illustrations where, almost invariably, as if *he* was the colonizer with a pair of prismatics slung round his neck, the parrot in question perches loftily concealed from view, a vast plain dotted with minute men laid out beneath him.[3] Bird-watching had also introduced me to the sequel to these colonial adventures: that fantasy of feathers that is the London Natural History Museum's dead bird collection. There, after closing hours, one supposes, the ghosts of Audubon's bird enemies still gather to shop for plumes, their hats coming to resemble the military cockades that somehow underwrote their opulence.[4] But my interest in parrots emerged after I had moulted these ornithological feathers: after migrating to Australia, one of seven realms that lay claim to the sobriquet 'Parrot Land',[5] although even there my parrots remained imaginary. I was amazed to find that the explorer Charles Sturt had based his hypothesis of an inland sea on his observations of migrating budgerigars.[6]

When I had overcome a growing articulation complex, I realized that my friends' sympathetic mishearings identified a new niche in the great eco-system of parrot enquiry, one I could occupy. Parroting back what they thought I had said, they translated my subject into something richly new. Mere parrotry invented new topics. Subsequently, plunging into the history of our fascination with parrots, I observed something else. Their flights of free cultural association were funny but, it transpired, far from arbitrary. They turned out to disclose a web of unsuspected connections. Parrots, it emerged, were a secret pattern woven throughout much of the fabric of our collective dreaming. Whether it was the macaws in Apollinaire's Parisian 'Les fenêtres',[7] Sparkie the champion budgie crying 'I love you, Mama' as he fell off his perch,[8] the ventriloquist's dummy or the prosthetic Polly making up for Long John Silver's missing leg: parrots were the secret sharer in human affairs. They could even teach English speakers a thing or two about articulation, an eighteenth-century traveller reporting that French parrots speak much more plainly than 'ours'.[9] And parrots performed their shadow role by rarely if ever acknowledging their own name: always slipping into other identities (Paris, parody), they were parasites, finding their identities in questioning ours.

Since all these discoveries had been made indirectly, in the human cage, as it were, without once directly addressing a parrot as 'Pretty Polly' or looking it in the eye, it was obvious that parrots could migrate down the pathways of the human imaginary without any reference to personally known parrots. I thought: when we put parrots in cages and teach them to talk,

Good pupil or guilty conscience? Graham Fransella's *Parrot's Revenge* of 1984, etching and aquatint.

it's a fantasy of communication with ourselves that we indulge. And something else (far more disturbing): if, as they say, parrots talk *only* in captivity,[10] what would be the consequence of setting them free? It would not be a triumph for the conservation movement, representing a kind of environmental post-colonialism, but the discovery that all this time we had been talking to ourselves. The mimetic charade in which parrots had indulged us had, in the end, disguised only an irremediable loss, our forfeited capacity to enter into the life of things, and so to save ourselves through them. The forest of parrot literature is dense with natural histories and cultural histories, but what it lacks is a history of parrots in communication that traces their counter-colonization of our collective verbal and visual imaginings. If ours has been a history of loving parrots to death, we need to cultivate a less deadly companionship. The first step is to confront a flock of psittacine fantasies.[11]

In this hand-coloured engraving from 1785, 'The Moment of Imagination', the dramatist Edward Topham thinks he has done something original. Looking at the parrot, the actress in the portrait, Mrs Siddons, knows better.

THE MOMENT OF IMAGINATION.

Parrots inhabit our cultures because they invade our imaginations. They represent the uncleared jungle of wish fulfilment. They populate a world where all parts speak to one another, and no transformation is prohibited. The poet Peter Steele imagines them more assertively, as colonists of the unconscious, 'in high feather/at taking by storm the mind's receding forest'.[12] But Steele calls his poem 'Dream Parrots'. Only in dreams, it appears, can we humans unlock the cage that binds parrots to our interests. Most histories of parrots ignore the role they play in the human imagination. Natural histories of parrots idealize

parrots, detaching them from an association with human interests that goes back to the Stone Age.[13] Their 'scientific' treatment of parrots masquerades as matter of fact, yet their taxonomies surface from a cultural undergrowth of explorers' tales,
collectors' fancy, mishearings and nostalgia.

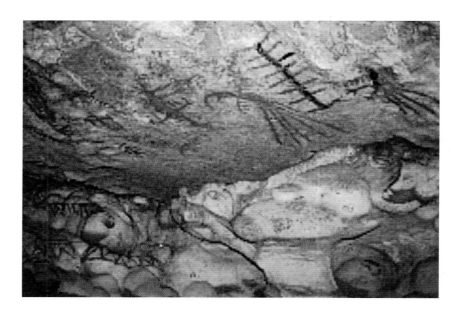

All beak, claws and tail feathers: dated between 3000 and 5000 BC, these cave paintings of macaws from Rio Grande do Norte suggest that parrots were dreamed before they were seen.

Natural histories fit the parrot family (all 353 species at the last count) into a grid whose axes are evolutionary and geographical. Scientific taxonomy is a vain attempt to preserve the notion of happy families. Cultural histories impose on their subject matter a no less fanciful grid in which a history of parrots in human culture (their introduction to the West is canonically ascribed to Alexander the Great) intersects with the variety of their usages at different places and times. The result is a classification of material quite as fanciful as anything the Argentinian novelist Jorge Luis Borges ever invented, in which Stone Age painted macaws, parrot-headed nebulae, Tang pots, Gary Larson cartoons, Lewis Carroll and Bette Davis keep strange company. Except for 'cockies' (small-scale Australian farmers who share their name with a parrot), every culture and

human type seems to have embraced parrots. They have no negative press. There is no anti-parrot lobby, no cat/dog division into pro- and anti-psittacines. They are honorary citizens of our fables and kitchens, poems and paintings, our real and dream zoos. Every human virtue has been detected in their look and comportment. Apart from vanity they escape every vice.

It's not simply their ability to talk that fascinates, but their talkativeness. Parrots like human company. They can be so keen on conversation that they forget to eat.[14] Parrots don't talk to each other, but they chat away to us.[15] All too human, they are more than human. They are knowing. They cast a 'cynic' eye on human affairs. Every beady-eyed parrot is a Diogenes, noting and mimicking our stupidity. We teach them to talk, and they add interest to their gain, talking back in tongues. A dictionary of quotations issues from their beaks, as if they know the secret correspondences between different languages. They conceal their proclamations inside riddles and metaphors, cage-perch orators. In the unexpectededness of their utterances, they are unconscious consciences. They bring a 'Cubist' dimension to the round table discussion. They fart, hiccough and cough in the middle of a Mozart aria. They tell old news. They ring up and answer the phone themselves. They amuse, they haunt, characterless, like actors. They stare back, listening. At night, under shrouds, they recall Paradise. Mocking familiars, they remind us of the road not taken. Polly is short for Melpomene. Muses that amuse, natural Parnassians, at the end they hop onto our shoulder, and rocking, swaying, genially guide us down to the underworld.

Into this Eden of cosy coexistence a chill breeze blows. Everywhere – and parrots are everywhere, on postage stamps, on windscreens, on church steeples, in wedding dances, in Monty Python sketches – they are disappearing. These sentences are punctuated by the groaning collapse of tropical trees, by the release of rocket nets, and the overnight delivery of drugged feather totems to foreign collectors. They had to be enslaved to be known. That much was clear. But that this slavery should prove fatal: this is too much to bear. It's not all joking with parrots. They are the bad consciences of colonialism. 'Flimsy and miserable,' Carroll thought them, 'something like a live mop'.[16] Mutated, in a few generations they look like ghosts.[17] Self-disgusted, they self-mutilate.[18] Patronizing parrots as the answer to our dreams – proof of 'intelligent life' out there – we have organized their genocide. Inside cages, they should have been safe from this. Bred to beguile the hours, television for the pre-televisual, they were our seers; and we have watched them to death.

The artist, Pieter Barbiers (1749–1842), largely copied parrots in the collection of the famous naturalist Coenraad Temminck. Considering the Sino-Tahitian landscape, the gigantic scale of the parrot and the impaled proclamation, will anything be *naturelle* about this history?

Parrot is divided into three chapters: Parrotics, Parroternalia and Parrotology. Parrotics presents an imaginary systematics, or classification, and, to make it a little less imaginary, information about parrot evolution, present-day appearance and distribution. This bias becomes less fanciful when one reflects on the fancifulness of scientific taxonomy. If the West has been a culture of 'splitters', keen to divide and subdivide birds into more and more species, other cultures, for no less scientific reasons, have been decisively 'lumpers', grouping parrots not only with other birds, but with animals, plants and even humans. Nor can the role that aviculture has played be overlooked: as fast as parrots have become extinct in the wild, fantasy flocks of mutants have increased in captivity. In this context, to identify an ur-parrot, a universal parrot type that seems to haunt humanity's collective dream, seems a relatively empirical step. I am not implying the existence of a universal archetype, simply describing a kind of parrot gestalt continually recharged by the circulation of stereotyped parrot icons and associations. Underneath the ur-parrot four genera of imaginary parrots can be identified: the Indian green Suka, the African Grey Psittacus, the Meso-American Guacamayo and the oriental Kakatua. These are the great world parrots. Once geographically distinct, although now caged together – the ur-parrot may have coalesced in the modern psyche after their mass export and global circulation had confused their distinct identities – they come down to us with diverse characters, associations, histories and powers.

Parroternalia is the body of *Parrot*. Its collection of parrot lore has the character of parrot plumage. At first it's hard to see what logic orders and links the different themes, yet gradually a pattern of repetitions and symmetries emerges. But this is true of the parrot's feather design: bilaterally symmetrical,

the colour patterns remain unpredictable. As it happens Parroternalia does fall into two halves, although they are hardly mirror images of each other. One tries to do justice to the human obsession with parrots talking; the other focuses on their polymorphic symbolism. Obviously it is artificial to separate these two strains of lore. Parrots function metonymically as erotic companions, angelic messengers, deceiving doubles and polymaths generally because of their mimetic powers. Parrots, however, are not only verbally mimetic: they copy us even when they are quiet. One symmetry that does emerge from this survey is a simple one. There is no quality attributed to parrot in one culture that is not contradicted in another. The question is whether the sage/fool, dumb/intelligent figure that emerges is simply an artefact of our panoptic survey, or whether his double nature is constitutional and informative.

Ferdinand Bauer, *Rainbow Lorikeets*, April 1802. At least twelve of Bauer's paintings that were made during Matthew Flinders's circumnavigation of Australia furnished the 'iconotype' on which the first scientific descriptions of new animals and birds were based.

Parrotology draws out, like the tail feathers of the macaw, certain leading motifs that emerge from the body of our parrot story. It is a quiver of reflections on our attempts to achieve a degree of parrot self-consciousness. Irene Pepperberg's long-time laboratory conversation with her African grey 'Alex' is exemplary, so are the efforts of some parrot fanciers, and a plethora of environmental conservation groups who, often under some threat to their own survival, fight for the protection of parrot habitats. But a certain reluctance to confront our psittacine fantasies persists. Parrot, whether in the laboratory or in the post-colonial forest, is still our subject. We remain avid to learn more about him, but reluctant to grasp what he teaches us. Or, to put it another way, perhaps the most surprising thing about parrots is not that they talk but that they listen.

1 Parrotics

Parrots come in 'all shapes and sizes'.

Joseph Forshaw[1]

And Forshaw should know. Even if his *Parrots of the World*, originally published in 1973, doesn't satisfy every parrot-watcher, it was the first global parrot guide, and remains an extraordinary achievement. So it's significant that, in the wake of that encyclopaedic survey, Forshaw still found the definition of the parrot family difficult: 'Systematists have always had difficulties classifying parrots and most arrangements proposed have been largely artificial.'[2] Now, the consensus is that parrots are easily distinguished from other bird groups (this confidence is quite recent): it is the internal family relations that are harder to sort out. Biochemical evidence suggests that parrot should be split into two families, the cockatoos (Cacatuidae) and the parrots (Psittacidae).[3] This leaves the lories and lorikeets, which some classify as a sub-family of the typical parrots, others as a family in their own right. Another guide to their evolutionary genealogy is geographical distribution, but here again there is less clarity than a taxonomist might desire. There are approximately 184 species of parrot in the Old World and 148 in the New.[4] But this division is probably less significant than the fact that there are 53 species in a dozen genera, all confined to Australasia, eastern Indonesia and many remote South Pacific islands, a fact whose evolutionary significance Alfred Russel Wallace first pointed out.[5] Despite a cosmopolitan

The convict-artist
Thomas Watling
painted this
'scarlet & green
parrot' (our King
parrot) in the
early 1790s at
Sydney Cove.
Why 'scarlet'?
Did Watling recall
the scarlet tunics
worn by the
soldiers who
caged *him*?

distribution round the tropics, parrots are confirmed islomanes. Their singularity and diversity of form are directly related to the profusion of islands.

These classificatory data may seem bland, but they stand at the edge of a historical jungle of taxonomic speculation. It was the voluminous eighteenth-century French naturalist Georges-Louis Leclerc, Comte de Buffon, who first separated the parrots of the Old World from the parrots of the New. But his reasons were marginally scientific. He subdivided these large families 'somewhat in accordance with the names they had received in popular language'.[6] This provokes an odd thought. Popular names tended to be imitative; even the parrot names that explorers got from the natives generally reproduced the calls of the birds themselves. Could it be that parrot taxonomy originated in families of sounds orchestrated by parrots? Perhaps it

was the same suspicion that parrots might be *intelligent* mimics that led the systematist C. L. Bonaparte to place parrots 'at the top of the class, conceiving that they were analogues of the Primates among mammals'. Nowadays they perch on a less elevated rung of the great avian hierarchy, a sub-order of the Cuculiform birds – although this association with cuckoos may also contain a folkloric substrate. As for the division of parrots into two families, it appears historically as an attempt to rein in the enthusiasm of older 'splitters', who by the end of the nineteenth century had 'discovered' enough anomalies in the type specimens laid out in museum drawers to generate no less than 500 parrot species. But, as the 1911 *Encyclopedia Britannica* contributor primly observed, most of these variations on the two-family scheme were highly artificial as 'any regard to osteology [the study of bones] would show'.[7]

Historically, the spatial distribution of parrots has been as hard to interpret as the evidence of family likeness. Anticipating Forshaw, John Latham, writing in 1776, puzzled over the fact that, while 'the genus consists of infinite variety . . . yet they seem to run vastly into one another, so as to induce one to think many of them related though received from different parts of the world'. Not having an evolutionary model to hand to account for the apparently global distribution of a parrot family, he offered an alternative explanation: 'we may be deceived, as they are perpetually carried from one continent to another for the sake of sale. This uncertainty of native place must prevent us following the otherwise judicious plan of *Buffon*, of ranging them according to the places they are supposed to inhabit.' John Latham proposed instead to 'divide them into those with *uneven*, those with *even* tails, much after the manner of *Linnaeus*'.[8] He had a point: 'The first significant effort to collect live animals on a scientific expedition did not occur until

The Horned
parrot from
New Caledonia,
illustrated in
John Latham's *A
General Synopsis
of Birds* (1776),
reveals itself as
belonging to the
'uneven' family
of parrots.

Nicolas Baudin's voyage (1800–1804).'[9] Prior to that parrots and other animals were taken on board 'as gifts, as commissions for the [French] king's menagerie, as commercial items, or as shipboard companions'.[10]

Students of parrots really had little idea where their birds came from: in 1751 the illustrator George Edwards explained that his 'Draught' of 'The Brazilian Green Parrot' was taken 'from the living Bird, at the sign of the Parrot and Cage, a Cage-Maker's in Crooked-Lane, London, who was also a dealer in Foreign Birds'. And he added 'He informed me that he bought it of one who brought it over from the Brazils.'[11] A yellow Amazon, depicted by Hulk, probably came from Brazil, he thought, because it spoke Portuguese.[12] In reality, the problem of provenance was even more complicated. As Errol Fuller suggests, science may never have known parrots in their natural habitat. If a seventeenth-century observer reported a blue and yellow macaw on a West Indian island, it was as likely to be an escaped pet as a new species.[13] Such displaced parrots Fuller calls 'anomalous'. Buffon's pre-modern nomenclature may not be without a certain value. The jacot of the *Histoire des animaux*, said to come from both India and Africa (and of which the commonest species is the grey Guinea [West African] parrot), may not yield to Linnaean classification, but it names one of the great world parrots, and preserves its human history, its perpetual carrying from one continent to another for the sake of sale.[14]

This little excursion into the backwoods of taxonomy illustrates the point that parrot systematics – the science of classification – is, and always has been, motivated. Buffon's conception of nature as 'an unbroken continuum or horizontal web (*réseau*) of inter-related beings whose connections could be described but never fixed in time, and where certain species acted as transitional categories or connectors between other larger – and more stable – categories of being' has a presciently ecological ring to it.[15] Linnaean taxonomy demanded a new way of looking and a new kind of subject. To constitute types or species, parrots had to possess a typical look. It followed that a system of classification based on external features needed to represent animals and plants typically. In the case of parrots, their polymorphism (variant forms) had to be repressed. At the same time, the extraordinary chromatic complexity of their plumage meant that they had (at least in the artist's representation) to be contorted into attitudes that would maximize their exposure. The poignancy of Edward Lear's unsurpassed parrot paintings undoubtedly stems from the new conditions of observation that Linnaean taxonomy imposed upon the scientific illustrator. The prismatic brilliance of the macaw's plumage, the hyper-real reproduction of individual feathers, communicates

The *Amazon jaune* or *Perroquet d'or*, published by Buffon in 1796, may have been the Yellow-naped Amazon parrot distributed along the Pacific coast of Central America, but Buffon chiefly valued his jacot for its prowess as a talker.

Psittacula torquata. 'There was an Old Man, on whose nose/ Most birds of the air could repose;/ But they all flew away'. Edward Lear was only 18 when he began his *Illustrations of the Family of the Psittacidae* (1832).

a profound anxiety. Breaking up the older family, science had created an avian orphanage. Lear wrote not only *for* children but *of* his children, when he versified: 'P was a polly/ All red and blue and green/ The most beautiful polly/ That ever was seen./ P! Poor little Polly.'[16]

Taxonomically speaking, Western science has divided in order to conquer. Other cultures have studied associations. As if differences were all too obvious, they have sought to blur them, in the process defining the meaning of family differently. Among the Arrernte of Central Australia, the plant called irriakura has the ring-necked parrot as its partner.[17] The adjacent Pitjantatjara people classify the same species differently. Their mountain-devil (Miniri) ceremony re-enacts how the smaller creatures gained their markings. 'The Ring-neck parrot, Patinpa, whom the bower-bird, Ikaraka, had decorated, was so pleased with his green plumage and yellow neck-band that he was anxious to make his partner as colourful as himself.' As it was getting dark, he lit a bunch of spinifex; but the fire got away. This explains why the plumage of certain birds is black.[18] Patinpa, in this culture, is not a 'parrot', but one of a family of animals small and harmless like the 7- to 13-year-old boys who dance their story.[19] The object of these 'marriages' is to bind the different parts of the world together and by joining them to make sense of them.

In contrast with us, these people group men and parrots together. In the twelfth century, John of Salisbury's castigation of anyone who imitated the parrot – 'They have shed the desirable element, their humanity, and in the sphere of conduct have made themselves like unto monsters'[20] – is representative of a strain of polly-nausea permeating two millennia of Western thought. Among many indigenous peoples of South America or Australia, I imagine it would be a monstrous thing to suggest that parrots were not human. But confusions of this kind are abhorrent to the scientific mind. 'The Bororos,' says Von den Steinem, who would not believe it, but finally had to give in to their explicit affirmations, 'give one rigidly to understand that they are araras [Scarlet macaws] at the present time, just as if a caterpillar declared itself to be a butterfly'.[21] Von den Steinem could not understand how these people, or at least his native informant, could believe themselves to be what they were not. The sociologists Durkheim and Mauss took it as an instance of a 'general mental confusion' found in 'the least evolved societies known', explaining that 'There is a complete lack of distinction between him and his exterior soul or his totem.' For 'the primitive', they generalized, 'the principle of *generatio aequivoca* [the confusion of opposites] is proved'.[22]

The confusion was all, of course, in the European mind, a consequence of imposing its 'violent categories' where they weren't wanted. One can merely repeat the point already made: an affirmation of sameness presupposes a recognition of difference. The ecological logic behind the Bororos' statement can be guessed at by referring to the rather better documented parrot beliefs of the Tzutujil Mayan people of Santiago Atitlan in Guatemala, among whom the parrot is identified as occupying a crucial position in the rain forest economy. The macaws, conures and Amazon parrots of the village follow the pattern of the maturing fruits and seeds from area to area, but they eat very little of what they tear off with their beaks, 'dropping to the forest floor ten times more than they actually eat'. Tapirs, *tepeizcuintes*, deer, peccaries and many ground birds follow the parrot flocks around; some of the hard jungle seeds consumed in this way sprout in the animals' dung and these fruit-eating vegetarian animals in turn attract meat-eating jaguars and other carnivores.[23] The parrot perched at the apex of a widening food pyramid; and it was natural to extend the parrot's benevolence

In this 8th-century 'wishing tree' from Prambanan, Java, horizontally paired this-world parrots are vertically paired with other-worldly bird-women or *kinnaras*.

to the provision of more distinctively human gifts. She 'was seen as a provider, a parent animal who teaches speech, feeds all the other animals, and instigates the replanting of fruit trees, all at one time'.[24]

In calling the Suka 'psittacus viridis', *The Art of Falconry* (*De arte venandi cum avibus*) of Frederick of Hohenstaufen, written around 1240, anticipated modern scientific nomenclature. The modern *Psittacus viridis* is the White-breasted parrot from Mexico.

In short, scientific taxonomy is one system of classification amongst many. And, despite its air of conceptual self-sufficiency, it is related to these older, pre-scientific systems. A 'typical sign' of the parrot is 'the big head with a bended strong beak'.[25] Even this seemingly obvious statement is the outcome of a long historical struggle to see parrots clearly. When Frederick II (1194–1250), first suggested that parrots could be classified by their beak shape, he was distinguishing like from like.[26] The Hohenstaufen emperor was an expert falconer. He owned an Umbrella cockatoo (presented by the Sultan of Babylon), but, so far as their beaks went, most of the parrots in his menagerie must have looked very like falcons. (To this day the identification of falcon glyphs, whether in Egypt or the Yucatan, is difficult.) But it's not simply that modern parrot systematics synthesize older systems, or that it is one system among many. It is the powerful *interests* these classifications represent that count. The oddity of our post-Linnaean attitude to animals is that it identifies the provision of knowledge with loosening the bonds of natural association.

Recycling nature or chain reaction? A parrot show at Woburn Abbey in England.

Animals are individualized, detached from their inter-specific flocks and their complex living arrangements. They are introduced into our intellectual cages (drawing-rooms, zoos and laboratories) as refugees from a war-torn zone. We master them to serve our interests, and it is in our interest to flatter our own intellectual vanity. The operatic, Hollywood brightness of parrots, no less than their equally deferential, neo-conservative chatter, are to some extent images of the world as we are taught to imagine it.

In this context, the resistance to classification that Forshaw mentions is not simply an obstacle to scientific tidiness: it is a critical mirror held up to it. The Argentinian fabulist Jorge Luis Borges allegedly found in a 'certain Chinese encyclopaedia' that animals were classified as (a) belonging to the emperor, (b) embalmed, (c) tame, (d) sucking pigs, (e) sirens, (f) fabulous, (g) stray dogs, (h) included in the present classification, (i) frenzied, (j) innumerable, (k) drawn with a very fine camel-hair brush, (l) *et cetera*, (m) having just broken the water pitcher,

(n) that from a long way off look like flies.[27] Borges's list has usually been taken to illustrate the arbitrariness of the frames we invent to reduce the world to order. Taking a genuine taxonomy, derived from a Chinese *leishu*, or reference book – in which the animal kingdom is reduced to fourteen kinds (including parrots, but also the phoenix, the dragon, tortoise, birds in general and the firefly) – Christoph Kaderas points out that, in the context of traditional Chinese literary education, these beasts were poetically related, all being known as good omens.[28] Perhaps the aim of Borges's list is less to show the

Parameters: parrot beaks and wings are turned into a system of curves in this polychrome jar of 2004 by the Hopi potter Stetson Setalla.

fantasies that different cultures invest in their families than to represent equivocation, for it is not only memory that modern science leaves out but the ambiguity of appearances. 'To be scientific means to be unambiguous.'[29]

Parrots defy classification not by coming in all shapes and sizes, but because they are chromatically mutable, promiscuously sociable, verbally equivocal and intellectually enigmatic. They are the supplement of creativity that slips through the net of systems designed to fix identity and function. Going back to Borges: has anyone pointed out that *one animal* exists that fits every category? I mean the parrot. Parrot certainly belongs to the emperor. Woody Allen tells a story about a parrot and pigs;[30] tameness is a noted parrot virtue;[31] they are innumerable; as for their brushes with brushes, as the Spanish poet Rafael Alberti remarks, 'Pinceles que son plumas/ azul añil, cuando de te se tiñen' ('Wings seize our brushes/ when we dip them in indigo').[32] The point is not simply that all taxonomies are partial and culture-bound. The polymorphic character of parrot brings into question the very idea of a single taxonomy. If 'parrot' is the name of whatever is 'included in this classification', then parrot is the name of what cannot be classified. Always equivocal, the concept of parrot makes a taxonomy of taxonomies possible, a parrotics.

UR-BIRD

From an evolutionary point of view, parrot may be the ur-bird. Whether you agree that the Archaeopteryx (Late Jurassic, *c.* 150 million years ago) is the 'grandfather' of the modern parrot,[33] may depend on what timescale of affinity you use. Alternatively, the parentage of parrot is entirely different, located among the few 'transitional' birds that survived the extinction

34

of the Cretaceous bird fauna about 65 million years ago.[34] A fossilized lower jawbone from eastern Wyoming, dated to the late Cretaceous, has 'nerve and blood vessel tracks identical to those of modern parrots'.[35] The oldest fossil parrot dug up in Great Britain postdates the Cretaceous, although more than 60 million years old, and was identified by its distinctive tibia bones.[36] The fact that parrots come in all shapes and sizes, from the 8.5-cm pygmy parrot to 100-cm macaws, and in colours varying from the dull brown of the Vasa parrot to the rainbow-hued sun conures and lories, suggests that their development began early.[37]

Parrot remains from the Miocene (24–5 million years ago) found near Allier in France, and dubbed by scientists *Archaeopsittacus verreauxi*, bore a resemblance to both the present-day African grey (*Psittacus erithacus*) and the Ring-necked parakeet (*Psittacula torquatus*).[38] The latter is among the most geographically widespread of all parrots, found from the mouth of the Gambia across Africa to the Red Sea, as well as throughout India, Sri Lanka, Myanmar and Thailand. The oldest representative of a modern genus, *Conuropsis fratercula*, comes from the upper Miocene (*c.* 20 million years ago) and is described from a left humerus found in Nebraska. Flying forward to within a million years of the present, representatives of two extant South American genera have been dug up in Ecuador and Venezuela.[39] The oldest *living* forms of parrots are thought to be in New Zealand, the kakapos, keas and kakas.[40] In any case, the polymorphism of different geographical groups, and the lack of intermediate types, suggests that the house of Polly is an ancient one.

So, too, does the pattern of their global distribution whose oddities, John Sparks and Tony Soper argue, reflect the migration of tectonic plates after the break-up of the massive prehistoric

Max Ernst, *Lop Lop* (c. 1931), oil on canvas. Why did Ernst call his 'mother superior of birds' Lop Lop? Is it Pol Pol backwards?

continent known as Gondwanaland. Parrots are pan-tropical birds with a distinct southern hemisphere bias. The greatest concentration of species (more than 200) is distributed southwards from Mexico, with more than 70 species found in Brazil. Approximately half this number is found in Australasia and the Philippines, but, in comparison with 'the comparatively homogeneous collection of species' from Central and South America, the Australasian parrots are 'an astonishingly diverse group'. This

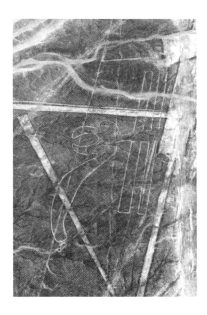

Paranormal? It is the existence of an ur-parrot gestalt that enables us to explain the production of this Nazca parrot geoglyph (Peru, c. AD 200–600) *without* recourse to Erich von Däniken-inspired extra-terrestrial visitors.

begs the question of which of these regions was the ancestral home of parrot: is Australasian diversity a sign of the antiquity of the line? Or does it reflect the fact that environmental changes in that region have been more extreme? In comparison with these two great centres of parrot evolution, only 34 kinds are reported from Africa, India and South-East Asia.[41]

Despite their polymorphism, parrots are easily distinguishable from other families of birds. So confident of this is 'Parrot Breeder', writing for the magazine *Australian Aviculture*, that he extracts from the empirical jungle of large and small, dull and bright, long-tailed and short-tailed parrots a Platonic type he calls 'the overall parrot', whose 'typical' features include the short, blunt, rounded bill with the curved upper mandible fitting neatly over the lower, a yoked (or zygodactylic) foot in which two toes point forwards and two back, a prominent peri-opthalmic region or eye-ring (featherless in some species), a fleshy cere (over the upper mandible) and a thick tongue (its resemblance to the human tongue explained, the ancient Greeks thought, why parrots could talk). The distinctiveness of parrots also resides in their mobility. The parrot's upper mandible is movable (in other families it is blocked to the skull), and the crosswise movement this permits gives great power and flexibility – beak and tongue together make a tool useful in cracking nuts, carving wood and digging holes. The parrot's zygodactylic gait is equally unmistakable. Parrot feet are designed to grip; they are made for the 'hand-over-hand' ascent and descent of ridged surfaces or rope-like twigs: on flat ground, parrots try to put one foot in front of the other, and appear to waddle. Not only are back-pointing and front-pointing toes on each foot 'yoked' together; it looks as if the parrot's short legs are manacled, and it creeps forward in chains. His waddling gait suggests a certain craftiness or guile. His seeming humility barely disguises an aggressive desire to dominate. Similarly, the black eye is 'beady', and resembles a passionately enlarged human pupil. The periopthalmic ring magnifies the look, conveying a knowing, wry expression.

In some respects parrots are extremely adaptable, in others remarkably conservative. If their evolutionary progenitor preceded the break-up of Gondwanaland, then the multiplication of parrot species tracked the fragmentation of the super-continent. Perhaps this not only accounts for their odd distribution but goes some way towards explaining why some parrot species have developed specialized needs, while others exhibit a cosmopolitan capacity to be at home anywhere. Attachment can be to local area (the Australian rock parrot nests exclusively under overhanging rocks overlooking the Great Southern Ocean) or to

Adapted for work, the bridled *psittaci* in this 3rd-century AD mosaic from Cologne have acquired a rake-like third forward toe as well as a burden of agricultural implements.

food source (the Hyacinth macaw of the Pantanal region of south-central South America largely depends on two species of palm nut). By contrast species like *myiopsitta* (quaker) or *psittacula* (ringnecks) not only thrive in captivity but, as escapees from cages, colonize cities and parks geographically and environmentally far removed from home.

Two further facts: with few exceptions all parrots large and small nest in hollows (in trees, termite mounds, river banks and cliffs, and, outside the breeding season, parrots are in general highly sociable – the animation of Australian cities owes much to the carnival fly-throughs of screeching flocks of lorikeets and parakeets. Does the persistence of these two traits tell us something about life 60 million years ago before Gondwanaland (and parrots) began to split apart? Does the parrot's odd combination of secretiveness and showmanship derive from an environment unlike ours, a humid, densely folded country invested with a giant, liana-festooned flora, characterized by narrow streaks of sky, flashes of dark water, and distances heard rather than seen – in which hollows, instead of being rare occurrences, formed in the joins between different surfaces? This might account for the obsessive behaviour parrots show in captivity, where they not only lack an adequate 'flock partner' (the human owner is a poor substitute) but the comforting complication of a world filled with hollows. Parrots in zoos fare even worse: a pair of Cloncurry ringnecks I watched in the Melbourne Zoo conducted an interminable inspection of the fine mesh wire forming the wall of their enclosure. Nibbling their way round the holes, checking for weak links, they looked as if they were trying to remember something, a world where hollows signified nests rather than the enigma of imprisonment.

Parrot comes in all shapes and sizes, but they are all recognizably one. Evolutionary accounts presuppose this, but so, it transpires, do cultural histories of parrots. When I began collecting information for this book, I quickly realized that most literary and popular references to parrots were non-species specific. Christopher Columbus's remark on making island-fall in the Caribbean, that 'I saw no beast of any kind in this island, except parrots',[42] was, as we shall see, motivated by extra-psittacid considerations, but in a way it is typical. Poets of Tang China or imperial Rome, parrot storytellers of all times and places, comedians and cartoonists, anthropologists, explorers and even cultural historians, rarely identify the 'parrot' of which they speak. The evolution of parrot in the poly-cultural imaginary inverts the order of its natural history. If, in the wild, over millions of years, parrots have assumed every shape and size, in the human domain the opposite has happened: the many have gradually coalesced into the one, and it is the *late* emergence of this parrot gestalt or universal type that proves

Red in tooth and claw? In Albert Tucker's *Armoured Faun Attacked by Parrots* (1969), even parrot souls cannot escape us, but remain impaled inside a cage of ringbarked trees.

the antiquity of our association with it. No doubt this phenomenon is partly an effect of translation: most of my sources are in English; few of their authors were ornithologists. But even the visual treatment of parrots tends to be generic. The great world parrots can usually be distinguished in Hindu temples, Benin sculpture or Mayan writing, but it is clear that the treatment is iconic. An instantly recognizable parrot-type exists.

The astonishing suggestion has been made that the first 'parrots' Columbus saw were stiff-winged shearwaters grooving the troughs of the Atlantic Ocean. (Later, his 'parrots' were probably Cuban Amazons in the Bahamas and, in Guadaloupe and Trinidad, 'spectacular macaws' – obviously, from a distance they all looked like flies.)[43] This quaintly raises the question posed by my own title: what does *Parrot* refer to? The etymology of the word is disappointing, as historically shallow as the evolutionary record is old. Medieval English *popinjay*, old French *pat'epaut*, German *pa-pagei*, Italian *pappagallo*, Spanish *periquito* or *periqueto*, French *perroquet* and *perruche* and English parakeet (variously spelled): this sounds like a family to me, but etymologists disagree, speculating that the first four terms are ultimately derived from the Arabic *Babagha* (the source of that word is unknown), while the remainder are a variety of diminutives of the proper name Pierre (French Perrot or Pierrot, the latter also being the familiar name in modern French of the house sparrow).[44] Spanish *periqueto* is the diminutive of *Perico*, a colloquial diminutive of Pedro, Peter. Parakeet is said to come from the Italian *parrochetto* (diminutive of *parroco*, parson) or else from Italian *parruchetto* (diminutive of *parruca*, peruke, periwig, in reference to the plumage of some species).[45]

Located beneath an image of the ten-armed Durga at Lakshmi-Janardan temple (West Bengal), the significance of these parrots is unknown. In Orissa the mother goddess is represented with a parrot-beak nose.

The same familiar condescension is observable in parrot's familiar names. English Polly or Poll and French Jacot or Jacquot fantasize an avian Harlequin (or Pierrot), a Tom Thumb, a household familiar, a not-too-particular serving maid, a slave. Poll or Polly is a familiar equivalent of Mary, altered from Moll, first recorded in 1630 with the sense of prostitute.[46] (The etymology of Jacquot is unknown: *Le Grand Robert de la langue française* thinks it is onomatopoeic of the bird's cry, or else a diminutive of Jacques.)[47] It is striking that Jacky and Polly were also the names preferred by colonizers, when christening their native subjects into hard labour or domestic service. Here, at least, men and animals *are* grouped. In the master-slave–conception of social relations that permeated every stratum of Europe's hierarchically structured societies, parrots go together with children and clowns, natives of that place, whores and wig-wearers.[48]

In Christian iconography, parrot is associated with Paradise (illustrated in Dürer's famous etching). On the one hand diminished, on the other parrot is built up. Perched on our shoulder like a spirit brother, he reverses roles, and accompanying us wherever we go, asleep or awake, 'squawking derisively . . . somersaulting gleefully upon my shoulder: "Who's a fat fraud, then?"' he cuts us down to size. Phil Smith, who described this experience in an article in *The Listener*, wasn't a parrot specialist, but this makes his testimony all the more impressive:

I have learnt to live with him now. He still shuffles along his perch at night, making sure I don't get a wink of sleep before some crucial event. At tender moments when you try to tie the tight little knot of love in your heart and tell her what you really feel, down he swoops from the trees, cackling in hollow mockery.[49]

In Albrecht Dürer's engraving *Adam and Eve* (1504), the Suka clings to a branch broken from the Tree of Life. As nature's artist she shares her perch with the artist's monogram. Notice that she is 'tame' here, because in Eden there is no need to be 'wild'.

The essence of the ur-parrot is its doubleness. The Polly/poly (Greek: many) pun is not trivial. Nor is it rare, confined to parrot-besotted researchers after a few drinks: scientists recently named the earliest fossil parrot found 'Pulchrapollia', punning on the Latin *pulcherrima* (very beautiful) and implying, I take it, that the one can contain the many.[50] Parrot originated double, as a one/many hybrid. This may account for their prominence among monsters. Apart from such familiar miscegenations as the parrot tulip and parrot fish, consider the parrot-beaked dinosaur or psittacosaurus or the scarcely less terrifying giant squid that attacks Captain Nemo's *Nautilus* in Jules Verne's *Twenty Thousand Leagues Under the Sea*. 'What a freak of nature, a bird's beak on a mollusc', Verne writes, correctly identifying the source of the almost atavistic revulsion the squid causes. 'The monster's mouth, a horned beak like a parrot's, opened and shut vertically.'[51] When a recently netted colossal squid made the popular press, the reports paid particular attention to its 'parrot-like beaks'.[52]

SUKA

Caged-bird experts assess the human 'compatibility' of the Indian parakeets as 'average',[53] but this seems ungenerous when it is considered that they have been in servitude since at least 398 BC, when a Greek physician first described seeing them at the court of the Persian king Artaxerxes II. His *Bittakos*, a bird that spoke the 'Indian' language naturally, as Ctesias thought, fits the species science knows as *Psittacula cyanocephala*, plum- or blossom-headed parakeet. Some think that Alexander the Great introduced the Alexandrine parakeet (*Psittacula eupatria*) to Europe – its name also commemorates the good country (*eupatria*) from which he comes. Yet others think that the bird that Aristotle kept as a pet and called Psittace was the Rose-ringed parakeet (*Psittacula krameri*). In any case any or all of these ring-necked parakeets belong to the green, or first great order of world parrots. From a Eurasian point of view, the green parrot comes from India, where he is known as the *suka* – from which the Greek word *psittakos* comes and *Psittacidae*, the parrot family's scientific name.

The parrot *vahana* or chariot, photographed by Sue Rees at the Kamakshi Amman Temple in Kanchipuram, Tamil Nadu, in 2002, is the preferred carrier of Kamadeva, the Hindu god of love, but he also uses the *Makara*, a capricorn-like crocodile – another sign of parrot's fishy connections.

As a trained pet bird with the faculty of speech, the green parrot or *suka* has figured in Indian folktales since Vedic times. His sauciness amused, and his native wit was admired. His paradoxically low high status is emblemized by his association with Kama, the Hindu god of love, who elevates him to his company only to treat him like a pack-mule, riding on his back. He also misses out on greatness in *The Buddha's Law Among the Birds*, where an anonymous seventeenth-century Tibetan monk anticipated modern parrot taxonomists in associating parrot with the cuckoo. But it is the cuckoo, or *kokila*, which the Buddha honours with his Dharma, even though the author may have followed an Indian tale where Prince Vikrama changed into a parrot.[54] Mediating between the Holy Lord Avakolita and the other birds, parrot is both their superior and cuckoo's inferior. He's a great go-between, but lacks leadership qualities; engaging, not charismatic. In folk tales he is gullible but educable. In one of the tales of *The Arabian Nights*, telling it the way he sees it proves fatal when his master grows tired of being corrected.[55] In the same vein, the *Jataka* tale 'How a parrot told tales of his mistress and had his neck wrung' apparently speaks for itself – except that there are two parrots in this story, and the second, a transformed Bodhisattva, has the wit to keep his beak closed until he has negotiated his freedom.[56] At his best, in Indian cultures, the green parrot is 'shrewd, cunning, faithful, self-sacrificing, fit for delicate missions, and capable of extricating men from difficult situations'.[57]

Kidnapped by Crusaders and brought to Europe, though, Suka is traded into slavery. He experiences loss of status, humiliation, violent re-education. In his history of writing and drugs, *The Road of Excess*, Marcus Boon cites a passage in which hashish is called 'green parrot'.[58] The eleventh-century Isma'ili Nizaris (identified in the medieval imagination of the West with the hashish-eating Assassins) were said to have a secret 'garden

In this illuminated Bible from Lisbon (1482), by the scribe Samuel ben Samuel ibn Musa, caged parrots are co-opted to the ornamental 'caging' of holy writ.

of paradise'.[59] Marco Polo's description of it does not name parrots, but the decor is consistent with their presence: 'the most beautiful palaces . . . of wonderful variety [were] gilded and adorned in azure very well with all the fair things of the world, both with beasts and with birds, and the hangings all of silk'.[60] Young men being recruited to carry out political assassinations were drugged twice, once to bring them to the paradise garden, to give them a glimpse of their reward, and a second time to take them out of it (for they would not have left voluntarily). Perhaps the drug that took them to paradise was named after the bird that lived there. Green parrot may transport you to its 'magnificent gardens and beautiful girls', but, when the imitation furnished by the hallucination begins to fade, it is

Toy angel? 'If a parrot can say Ave, why could not a young girl give life to Jesus after the Ave of the Angel Gabriel?' (Franciscus de Retza, 1426). On this basis the Suka depicted by Jan van Eyck in his *Virgin and Child with Canon Joris* (1436) is said to symbolize the Annunciation.

implicated in the fall. Because of their cloistered upbringing, they seem unaware of the frustration that Paradise Lost creates, and its corollary, a desire parrots should be caged as we are. 'Popyungayes froo Paradys comyn al grene', as the Tudor poet John Lydgate put it, in a double sense.[61]

How else to explain the statement, furnished by Pliny the Elder, that the green parrot's 'head is as hard as its beak; and when it is being taught to speak it is beaten on the head with an iron rod – otherwise it does not feel blows'.[62] 'A parrot's beak is so hard,' White's *Bestiary* explains, 'that if you throw down the

48

bird from a height on a rock, it saves itself by landing on its beak with its mouth tight shut, using the beak as a kind of foundation for the shock.' The reason for this fall is the parrot's fallibility. 'Although it really does try to copy what its teacher is saying, it wants an occasional crack with an iron bar.'[63] No wonder Greek hoplites (soldiers) carried parrots into battle: with skulls like that, who needed armour? The belief informing this primitive version of electric-shock therapy was, as Aristotle put it, that 'all birds with crooked talons are short-necked, flat-tongued, and disposed to mimicry'.[64] In addition, the Indian parrot was said to be endowed with 'a man's tongue'.[65] The pedagogical challenge was to activate that disposition and loosen that tongue. Apuleius who, like a number of Roman writers, cast our by now dazed and tongue-lolling subject in the role of the inferior or imitative poet, explained that even the well-trained bird 'can only "parrot" what others have taught it. If you teach it how to curse, cursing is all it will do. And if you want to get rid of it, you have to cut out its tongue, or let the bird fly to its native woods.'[66]

Apuleius was wrong. Green parrots can easily be retrained. 'They are not as good at talking as some of the larger parrots, such as the African grey, but many will learn at least a few words', a companion bird consultant explains understandingly.[67] This may explain why the Romans do not appear to have regarded the parrot's talking skills as particularly exceptional – the magpie was said to talk 'more articulately'.[68] The caged-bird counsellor continues: 'They may be shy when they initially enter your home, but with time, patience, and regular handling they should become tame quite easily.'[69] The charming creation of the eighteenth-century writer Jean-Baptiste-Louis Gresset, Ver-Vert, the Nunnery parrot, is 'retrained' during his return journey from another monastery. Loaned on account of his reputation for exemplary piety, wisdom, eloquence and the ortho-doxy of his beliefs, Ver-Vert picks up the language of the boatmen transporting him home. Punished, purged of his bad language, and again retrained, Ver-Vert regains the nuns' affections, only to die of an overdose of candy.[70] Ver-Vert is one of a flock of literary parrots whose powers of imitation expose human 'parrots': in contrast with the emotionally supple Ver-Vert, observant, diplomatic and adaptable, the humans who control his destiny are mired in superstition and custom. Even so, compared with his Indian cousins, the French parrot lacks agency: the irony of the situation is of the author's making, not his.

Ver-Vert's most significant attribute is his name. Why 'Green Worm'? 'Ver vert' furnishes the opening phrase of a French tongue-twister. It hints at half the truth (*verité*). It suggests a stutter in need of tongue-loosening. It is also a repetition that doesn't quite repeat itself, in which a tiny difference opens up. It hints at the green parrot's double nature. Ver-Vert may have nothing of his own to say, but he doesn't quite talk like anyone else. When several nuns questioned him at once, he answered each in their own way.[71]

As a world parrot type, the green parrot has long ceased to be confined to India. His kind is, for example, widespread throughout Australia. Nowadays, his best-known, globally distributed avatar is the budgerigar.

As many as 3,000 Rose-ringed parakeets (*Psittacula krameri*) can be found in south London, England. The parakeets may have descended from captive birds escaped during the 1950s and 1960s. They live at high altitudes on mountains in India, so can tolerate British winters. The Central Science Laboratory is monitoring the birds because they are a pest in India, and pose

Elizabeth Gould died in childbirth in 1841, aged 37. In the twelve years of her marriage she produced 600 lithographs for John Gould's *The Birds of Australia*. The birds the Goulds took back to England are said to be the ancestors of the now universally popular 'budgie'.

problems for orchard farmers. The London colony has yet to show a desire to migrate to the countryside.[72]

PSITTACUS

Parrot's double nature is not simply a discovery of the imagination. It is a historical fact. The parrot in captivity is a different species from the parrot in the wild. The schizophrenic world of

Psittacus, our second great world parrot, illustrates this nicely. Psittacus, following scientific taxonomy, refers to the African grey parrot (*Psittacus erithacus*) – the Greeks and Romans applied the same term to their green or Indian ring-necks. Our imaginary Psittacus also includes, though, the Amazons of the Caribbean and South America, who resemble the African grey in general shape, and in their verbal flair.[73] Whether via the Portuguese from West Africa, or on Spanish ships from the New World, Psittacus arrived in Europe at the beginning of the sixteenth century as a trade object. Columbus brought back from his first Caribbean voyage a pair of Cuban Amazons for Queen Isabella of Spain. Henry VIII's African grey was part of English folklore. Habitually perched overlooking the Thames, it picked up the chatter of watermen and their passengers; so when it fell into the water one day, it knew what to do, squawking 'A boat! Twenty pounds for a boat.' The waterman who answered its call created a ticklish problem for its absolute owner when he demanded the reward.[74]

In this context, *Azor, the Enchanted Prince* by the Abbé Du Guay de Launay (1750) is a missed opportunity. An island populated by mutes is taught to speak by a parrot. It is a disappointment to learn that the parrot is only a metamorphosed prince. Psittacus has been known to preserve human speech after its last speakers have died.[75] Its capacity to answer rationally puzzled the philosopher John Locke.[76] It would be less of a fairy tale to entertain the possibility that our speech is copied from Psittacus. This would explain why the bird seems to have such a well-developed sense of humour. Buffon reports 'a Parrot, which, when a person said to it, "Laugh, Poll, laugh," it laughed accordingly; and, immediately after, screamed out, "What a fool! To make me laugh".'[77] Buffon, still Psittacus's best domestic biographer, says that his sister's parrot 'would frequently speak to himself, and seemed to fancy that someone addressed him'.[78] Perhaps he recognized that mere mimicry is always a parasite on events outside its control. Like Bob Dylan's 'camouflage parrot' ('he flutters from fear/ when something he doesn't know/ about suddenly appears/ what cannot be imitated perfect/ must die'),[79] he wanted to perfect his representation of human speech by imitating the conversation with oneself that often passes for conversation with another.

Psittacus is an allegorical creature, a master of other speak. These discoveries are speculative in comparison with the scrupulously checked, minutely documented and quantitively, as well as qualitatively, impressive findings Irene Pepperberg has made about the African grey's intelligence. Like an anthropologist getting the local language, her success has depended on a cooperative 'native informant'. Alex's astonishing ability to do what are, in effect, intelligence tests gives a novel sense to the

Putting its best foot forward: this mid-18th-century engraving poses an African grey, a familiar cage bird, on a lonely tree stump.

classical artist's vaunt of holding up a mirror to nature since, in the process of reflecting on the tasks given to him, Alex has also allowed Pepperberg to reflect on *his* nature. His 'abstract aptitude' is illustrated by his capacity to comprehend the concept of 'category'. He can 'understand that "green", for example, is a particular instance of the category "colour"'.[80] Alex must be the first parrot who could, in principle, recognize that he is not a (green) parrot, and communicate this fact to us. Alex had to be excluded from Pepperberg's study of how greys respond to mirrors because 'long before this project was initiated, he had essentially been taught that the image he saw in the mirror was "Alex"'.[81]

The solitary confinement to which we condemn Polly née Psittacus now has real world implications. Scientifically trained zoologists have often treated aviculturalists with disdain, but in the case of many species of parrot, they have to rely on them for information about nesting. When conservationists seek to repopulate habitats decimated by the activities of bird-trappers, they develop 'strategies that will preserve wild populations [of African grey parrots] and their habitats' on the basis of *laboratory* studies of the bird's 'intelligence and extraordinary mimetic abilities'.[82] Even if the 'species' are only behaviourally differentiated, how, when they are returned to Paradise, will they communicate or understand each other? As Polynesia explains to Stubbins,

> I may have started the Doctor learning [animal languages] but I never could have done even that, if he hadn't first taught me to understand what I was saying when I spoke English. You see, many parrots can talk like a person, but very few of them understand what they are saying.[83]

The stage star Lola Montès (1818–1861) and her show-off pet. Since Lola, Lou Lou and even Lolita are favoured parrot names, the imitation is near perfect.

A recent report states: 'Scientists are trying to increase [a] captive population [of St Vincent Amazon parrots] not for reintroduction purposes [but] as a reinforcement to those in the wild.'[84] Perhaps this merely recognizes that Psittacus has always inhabited a parallel universe.

GUACAMAYO

Although Suka and Psittacus are sharply differentiated morphologically, and circulate in our collective imaginary with dif-

Georg Flegel (1566–1638), *Still Life with Parrot*, oil on copper. Is the Amazon part of the sensuous spectacle or a wry commentary on our visual gluttony?

ferent symbolic associations, they have much in common. Their companionability and mimetic gifts are shared with the third great world parrot, classically imagined in Europe as the Scarlet macaw, but associated in Fourth World and Meso-American consciousness with the name Guacamayo, and after whom a score (possibly many more) towns and villages in Colombia are named. Like Suka, Guacamayo has been ruthlessly exploited for the caged bird-market. A wild population of at least 50,000 Hyacinth macaws found in Paraguay and Brazil has been reduced to an estimated 3,000 today. The practical extinction of the Spix macaw is only the most dramamtic among many tales of human greed, vanity and bloody-mindedness.[85]

When not exterminated, Guacamayo is mutated. The fifteen or more species of macaw found throughout the American neotropics are easily recognized – 'remarkable for their gaudy plumage, which exhibits the brightest scarlet, yellow, blue and green in varying proportion and often in violent contrast, while a white visage often adds a very peculiar and expressive character'[86] – but less easily split into species. Taxonomists dispute the relationship, or difference, between the blue macaws – *Ara hyacinthinus, A. leari, A. glaucus* and *Cyanopsittacus spixi*.[87] Aviculturalists, fascinated by Guacamayo's polychromatic invention, have invented a few new parrots of their own. In Utah the progeny of a pair composed of a *hyacinthus* and an *ararauna* (Blue and gold macaw) looked like the former from the back, the latter from the front. Crosses with Scarlet and Green-winged macaws have brought poor returns, their offspring being described as 'large, purple and ugly'.[88]

Mutable as Suka, Guacamayo has been as mobile as Psittacus. Dead or alive, he has been the trade parrot par excellence. He is the most widely distributed parrot in European painting. In the Cantino World Map (1502) he perches on Venezuela as an emblem of South America. In the same decade, the trade in macaw and other parrot feathers had earned Brazil its sobriquet 'land of parrots'. He is found in greatest abundance, not in the rain forests of Surinam, but in the painted ceilings of Rococo Dresden, Gobelins tapestries and two generations of Dutch portraits 'with parrot'. He symbolizes political power, conspicuous consumption. On the arm of a Venetian senator, he is a post-colonial time bomb waiting to go off. Accompanied by a native servant, he signifies negritude. Rilke writes of zoo parrots: 'balanced on perches that silently rock with their yearning/ they breathe in

The petroglyph macaw from Anazazi National Monument, New Mexico, preserves the memory of a species long extinct locally.

In S. Manetti, L. Lorenzi and V. Vanni's *Storia naturale degli uccelli* (1767), the parrot is identified as 'the Green Macaw from Brazil', but the Great green macaw species (*Ara ambigua*) comes from Costa Rica, where its numbers are now reduced to double figures.

57

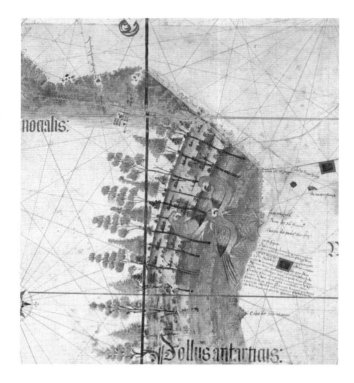

noaalis:

Sollus antarnais:

the alien air, always remembering/ their homeland'.[89] But Guacamayo's resentment is anything but elegiac: like Rilke's panther, he mutinously bides his time. Louise E. Robbins says that in pre-revolutionary Paris nobles 'let their scarlet macaws fly about, because they were tame and would return home. Several lost-and-found notices indicated that the lost parrot had a few links of chain attached to one foot.'[90]

This reminds me of Dr Thornton's blue macaw, 'Like others of his tribe . . . chained by the leg'. In this condition, he learned to talk but persisted in 'those screaming noises so offensive in his tribe'. When 'from motives of humanity as well as for experiment', his chain was removed, his vocal behaviour underwent a renovation. As tottering on weak, cramped feet yielded to a more confident prancing, so with his talk and manners: 'He soon forgot his barbarous sounds, and imitated words; and for hours together amused himself in saying "Poll," – "Maccaw," – "Turn him out," – "Pretty fellow," etc.' Tamed in this regard, the macaw showed a surprising freedom of invention: he imitated the scissors-grinder by grinding the upper mandible of his beak against the lower one, and observing the timing of the turning of the wheel struck his perch with his claws.[91]

In his homelands Guacamayo enjoys the status of a god. He is one of the Quecholli, or Thirteen Fliers, in pre-Colombian Mexican culture. One of the creations in the Mayan Popol Vuh centres on Seven Parrot and his family, identified in some codices with the macaw.[92] Near the Copán Valley in Honduras, the people named their most sacred area 'Macaw Mountain'; one month of the year, 'Muan', is indicated by the sign of a bird's head; the founder of a dynasty of kings was called Yax-Kuk-Mo, which means 'Blue-quetzal-macaw'.[93] His descendant is the trickster god Guacamayo in Miguel Angel Asturias's theatrical phantasmagoria, Cuculcan, where, as the 'Great Saliva of the Mirror', he embodies linguistic deceit and impurity.[94] Among the Mekranoti, Kaiopo, Bororo, Tukano and other Amazonian peoples, he is an other-worldly messenger. To wear his feathers and those of other brightly coloured birds is to absorb his creative energies.

But reverence does not mean respect:

At dawn, I got up to go out and visit the village; at the door I tripped over some pathetic-looking birds: these were the domesticated macaws which the Indians kept in

Head-dress from the Amazon basin: poignant proof that human narcissism is universal.

the village so as to be able to pluck them alive and thus obtain the feathers they need for the head-dresses. Stripped of their plumage and unable to fly, the birds looked like chickens ready for the spit and afflicted with particularly enormous beaks since plucking had reduced their body size by half. Other macaws, whose feathers had regrown, were solemnly perched on the roofs like heraldic emblems, enameled gules and azur.[95]

This passage from Levi Strauss's *Tristes tropiques* remains a poignant image of what, in another context, companion parrot advisors call the parrot 'misery index'.[96]

In 'Child with a Cockatoo', meditating on a seventeenth-century painting ('Portrait of Anne, daughter of the Duke of Bedford by S. Verelst'), the Australian poet Rosemary Dobson imagines this parrot coming from 'fabled shores' yet to be colonized. It is more likely that he was picked up in Indonesia. A century or so later, Louis Antoine de Bougainville reported that the going rate for a cockatoo in Malaysia and Indonesia was one red handkerchief.[97] Jules Dumont D'Urville's cockatoo companion got out of its cage and broke his barometer. Carried to New Guinea, it excited interest among the natives as a novelty – a rare instance of the parrot trade reversed.[98] But Dobson's parrot possesses a knowledge that no one can receive: 'So many years to come and still, he knew,/ Brooded that great, dark island continent/ Terra Australis . . . Terra Australis, unimagined land – / Only that sulphur-crested bird could tell . . . '. He signifies the future, but his significance is overlooked – perhaps this is why 'the curious bird' keeps its 'cynic eyes half closed'. The pathos of this 'old adventurer' is that he is 'a sign unread'. He is a signified but not a signifier. He has, presumably, a natural history; he has, as the painting shows, a cultural history. What he lacks, Dobson implies, is a place in the human

In this 9th-century bas-relief from Prambanan, Java (possibly the earliest represent-ation of parrots in Asian temple architecture), the cockatoos are already cast as pure ornament.

imaginary. His pathos is that as yet he symbolizes nothing. For a sign that is unread is nothing at all.

The large canvas *Triumph, with Treasures of East and West,* inside the main hall or Oranjezaal of the Huis ten Bosch (outside The Hague), identifies the treasure of Brazil with a scarlet macaw, while a sulphur-crested cockatoo rides the pile of precious objects collected from the East. In the battle of imperial emblems, his chief asset was probably yellow head feathers that could be erected to look like the rays of the rising sun. The abundance of parrots that the British found when they colonized Australia, the variety they trapped, caged, traded, painted, skinned and stuffed, suggested that 'Regio psittacorum', the enigmatic legend on Gerardus Mercator's World Map of 1537, had been another sign unread. After that, Kakatua developed, if the poet Chris Wallace-Crabbe is believed, a post-colonial consciousness. It is Puck, the unofficial spirit who disembarks with the official party at Sydney Cove, intent on rewriting 'Empire as larrikin culture', who first recognizes the cockatoo as his soul (and perhaps cell) mate: 'Against the pale enamel sky/ Rebel cockatoos are screaming/ New versions of pleasure:/ This is the paradise of Schadenfreude.'[99]

Anthropomorphic White cockatoo dreamings from Mennge-ya, NorthernTerritory, Australia, maybe an early Aboriginal response to land tenure threats.

Once a sign unread, now in Australia the cockie is read everywhere. As Kakatua he gives his name to an oil-field in the Timor Sea, as White Cockatoo to 'Australasia's Premier Nudist Resort' and to an indigenous performance group. There is a cockatoo screensaver and a Cockatoo Brand (see crate labels, T-shirts, coasters, mouse pads, ceramic tiles, wood plaques, etc.) Because of its convict associations (or to exorcise Puck), the Sydney Harbour Federation Trust has recently renamed Cockatoo island 'Biloela' – 'Aboriginal for cockatoo' (*sic*).

A fossilized beak found at Riversleigh in north-western Queensland indicates that the Kakatua was thriving in Australia in the early Miocene period (23–16 million years ago).[100] The non-indigenous name for this parrot, though, is Malay, and is said to mean either 'pincher' (think again of those female fingers thrust through the bars, inviting a nip) or 'old father', which recalls his descent from the 'All Father' ur-parrot.[101] Kakatua is famously long-lived which, Dobson implies, makes the 'old adventurer' 'wise as Time'.[102] Lady Anne Fanshawe recorded that in 1645 she saw 'at Mr Palmer's where we lay [at

Cockatoo as Baroque chicken in Aldrovandi's *Ornithologiae* (1646); it is possible that Gian Lorenzo Bernini had a hand in this concoction.

Barnstaple, Devon] a parrot above an hundred years old'. Another cockatoo, captured during the Indian Mutiny, 'was present in every action in which the regiment was engaged, surviving the campaign without a scratch, although a round shot took off the head of the bearer first appointed'. He subsequently 'passed a tranquil and fairly blameless life' in England, dying in March 1908. Nor is this longevity outstanding: a parrot living in Swindon, Wiltshire, in the 1920s had once belonged to a sometime Governor-General of India, Warren Hastings, who died in 1818. It is not recorded whether this imperial fowl spoke Hindi, but a parrot that lived in an English family for 53 years 'swore emphatically in Portuguese'.[103]

The truth is that his superhuman longevity produces disappointing results: Kakatua may have seen beyond the horizon of human mortality but what he can tell us about what he has seen is, like the news from the other side that the seance medium transmits, trivial. Despite his alarming crest and noisy manners, the cockatoo is pacific: 'Carrying or wearing white cockatoo feathers is a sign of peace when arriving at a stranger's camp.'[104] Like Jacot, he mourns when one of his own kind is shot.[105] The colonial explorer and administrator Sir George Grey reported that the Aborigines took advantage of this trait: having brought down one of more cockatoos with his kiley or boomerang,

> the wily savage has not yet done with them. He avails himself of their extraordinary attachment which these birds have for one another, and fastening a wounded one to a tree, so that its cries may induce its companions to return, he watches his opportunity, by throwing his kiley or spear, to add another bird or two to the booty he has already obtained.[106]

64

To judge by their vernacular names, the 'cockies', or smallholder Australian farmers, must, like the South American Bororos, think they are parrots, but this doesn't produce a sentimental attachment. The Western Australian Environment Minister recently warned farmers that they risked fines of up to $A 10,000 if they killed either Carnaby's or Baudin's cockatoos (both threatened species) in an effort to prevent damage to orchards and crops.[107]

Affectionate, socially inept, excitable and vulgar, Kakatua is a natural vaudeville performer.

The cockatoo is highly intelligent and their ability to repeat some words or sounds can be accomplished with

The master modeller Johann Joachim Kändler based this Meissen porcelain creation (1734) on captive birds he had studied in Moritzburg.

repeated training, but this is not the cockatoo's strength. Their outstanding ability comes from being great performers. This is demonstrated by such antics as dancing, playing tug-of-war, climbing, and shaking. They will use 'tools', various objects and toys to play and perform with, such as roller skating.[108]

These are the four great world parrots. Identifying them does not throw a comprehensive net over the 300-odd parrot species known world-wide. Only the alliteratively inclined – or an advocate of the 'bow-wow' or onomatopoeic theory of the origins of language – would place the Kakapo, Kea or Kaka in the Kakatua tribe; the wonderful Australasian parrots exhibit a prismatic invention that is hallucinatory, an Indian excess one might say, in comparison with which the Indian Suka is tame. Equally, our imaginary types hardly throw light on the ticklish relations between macaws and conures, or for that matter establish ground rules for calling parrots 'conures' at all. Is Spix's macaw more closely related to the Peach-fronted conure than to the Blue and yellow macaw?[109] It is, sadly, academic.

But it is time to leave the clearing and plunge into the jungle. Sensitive readers need not be anxious about the colonizing image. Not should they fear that it's all sobs: we may be laughing ourselves to death, but the way is punctuated with the most surprising asides, timely jokes and erotic intrigues. The jungle of Parroternalia is remarkably like the contemporary electronic city. It is the cultural niches that parrot signs occupy in our global communication network that are exposed.

2 Parroternalia

According to a news report from Brisbane, Australia, a Sulphur-crested cockatoo called Fritz has recently 'out tipped veteran rugby league tipsters and former players Warren and Choppy. His owner, Natalie, says Fritz is also a dab hand at AFL tipping, but what everyone wants to know', is, the report adds, 'Can he pick this week's lotto numbers?'[1] Fritz's fifteen minutes of fame as a talkback star is hardly exceptional. Besides advising punters, telling fortunes and oversighting lotteries – in the Pennsylvania Cash Quest Instant Lottery Game, parrot is a 'Key Symbol' of the 'Treasure Map'[2] – they promote colour photocopying, prudent investments, hair replacement therapies, get-away weekends and, inevitably, long-distance phone deals. Purveyors of empty promises, parrots are advertising's natural mascot.

'In art the parrot became the symbol of prophecy', a learned contributor to *Notes and Queries* once wrote, with reference to the green parrot's medieval association with the Mother of God, and the semi-divine prescience bestowed on her by her household familiarity with the arbours, avenues and gazebos of Eden, but he spoiled the effect by adding: 'which is perhaps not very polite to the seer'.[3] Perhaps it is not very polite to the parrot. The successful prophet knows how to throw the dice, rather

Macaw gimmick:
the lottery of the
democratic will.

than calculate their fall. In this, parrot is an able assistant. Parrots trained to pick out tarot cards used to be a common sight in India. In a report from Tamil Nadu, the 'colourfully dressed' tarot reader carefully spread his cards on a red cloth and opened the door of the wooden cage:

> The little green parrot hopped out strutting towards the cards. It pulled each card aside and eventually picked one with its beak and gave it to the man. He took the card in his hand and gave the parrot its reward with the other – a rice grain. The parrot strutted back obediently into its cage with the grain in its beak. The man now opened the card and proceeded to interpret the symbol.[4]

68

If Robert Hughes's description of Joseph Cornell as 'reclusive, grey, long-beaked' is accurate, this box construction of 1953–4 – whether its proper name is *Untitled* or *A Parrot for Juan Gris* – was very much a personal gift.

Even if it performs mechanically, a parrot produces unexpected results. However exact a mimic, it introduces chance. Amin Khan Pathan, a parrot trainer in Vadodara, tells a good story. His parrots 'can fire a cannon, play the piano, operate cameras, thread beads, use the tiny merry-go-round, rotate a ball of fire and even detect counterfeit coins'. He recalls the parrot show his great-grandfather put on for the Viceroy, Lord Minto. The parrots were performing the cannon trick, producing explosions that could be heard 2 km away. 'The security guards, suspecting a coup, rushed in to find Lord Minto laughing instead. He was amused that a small bird like a parrot had scared his soldiers.'[5] As the historical sequel proved, the laugh was on Lord Minto.

As for *hearing* future explosions: Eugene Linden cites Sally Blanchard, a parrot psychologist no less, who reports that her birds 'started screaming about fifteen minutes before the big San Francisco quake of 1989, and that after the quake she had a flood of calls from parrot owners saying that their birds had begun freaking before the trembler hit'.[6] This raises an interesting question: why didn't Blanchard's prescient parrots address their foster parents, talking rather than squawking?

Astrology places these avian messengers in the house of Hermes. As a mercurial type, parrot is grouped with birds that are 'naturally witty, melodious, and inconstant',[7] hardly sufficient information to interpret a parrot in one's horoscope. But wait: 'Things under *Mercury* are these; amongst Elements, Water, although it moves all things indistinctly; amongst humours, those especially which are mixed, as also the Animall spirit.'[8] Marry these qualities, and a Piscean emerges. The Piscean

is not infrequently thriftless, and when in difficulties a parasitic element may arise. If you want a good portrait

of our sign in modern literature, turn to Wells' Mr Polly.
To begin with, the name is Piscean, for it suggests a
parrot, and this loquacious bird is certainly Piscean.
Natives of the sign often look like parrots . . . [9]

Otherwise, the general rule is: if parrots fly through your
dreams, beware of flattering strangers.

One of the features of a universe (or a story) where anything
happens, is that the phenomenon of repetition acquires a meaning. For, in a game governed by chance, the repetition of what
has gone before seems subjectively the least likely of events. This
happened to our reporter in Tamil Nadu. He approached three
different tarot readers that day. On every occasion the parrot

Symbolic excess:
the French Art
Deco artist Jean
Dupas exhibited
Les Perruches at
the 1925 Paris
Exhibition. If this
is a dream vision,
it is a nice touch
that most of the
lovebirds are also
asleep. Oil on
canvas.

The subaltern speaks: Ram and his mother with parrot (Chitrashala Press, Poona, 1880s).

picked out the same card, an occurrence so unlikely that he thought it illustrated Jung's principle of 'Synchronicity, a-causal meaningful coincidences'. Jung never developed this notion in detail but one writer says: 'it was an idea that always seemed to sit on his shoulder like some faithful old parrot'.[10]

And with good reason, to judge from another Jungian anecdote. A man who was bored with a bar mitzvah ceremony he had to attend began to read a book of fairy tales. He 'found one about a white parrot which guarded the source of life, and anyone who reached for it in the wrong way was turned to stone', and suddenly recognized its relevance to his own attitude to the bah mitzvah. 'At that moment he heard a cawing outside, and looked up to see a white parrot in a bush outside his window.'[11]

Parrots may bring you face to face with your future. They also bend the prison bars of time past, appearing as prophets of what has already been lost. In this guise they are remarkable not for imitation, but for being inimitable. Two minutes fifteen seconds into Fernand Léger's film *Ballet Mécanique* a cockatoo appears, 'turning to face the camera and then turning away. It disappears in a flash of light and is not repeated.' In 'a film composed of repetitions and enlargements of everyday life', the conventional symbol of facile reproduction is the one image not copied, reproduced, repeated. Why? John Berger suggests that it signifies the momentary irruption of 'nature' – 'Time is real; the bird appears and is gone. In the context of the collage it is a heart beat in a world of artificial drumming . . . Trapped in the ballet, the bird returns to time, to nature.'[12]

This, though, is a symbolic role any bird could play. In post-Revolutionary Paris, as Elaine Robbins shows, parrot represented nature denatured. Cockatoos were cage birds and circus performers. They were part of the noise of everyday modern life:

You read handbills, catalogues, posters that shout out loud. Here's this morning's poetry, and for prose you've got the newspapers. Sixpenny detective novels full of cop stories. Biographies of big shots, a thousand different titles. Lettering on billboards and walls. Doorplates and posters squawk like parrots.[13]

Trapped inside the cage of representation, Léger's cockatoo is a media image, belonging to the same tradition as Fritz the tipster. He is 'society', the crowd.

Berger's sense of a bird entrapped may arise from the fact that it represents a *lost* society. I would place Léger's cockatoo in an anecdotal series that begins with John Locke's story about the old parrot 'celebrated for answering like a rational creature',[14] includes Humboldt's famous encounter with 'a venerable bird who had the sole knowledge of a dead language, the whole tribe of Indians (Atures) who alone spoke it having become extinct',[15] and resurfaces in Hergé's Tintin comic book adventure, *Red Rackham's Treasure*, where the parrots preserve a miscellany of long defunct mariners' curses.[16] Locke's story, which occurred during the government of Prince Maurice in Brazil, is usually taken (as the philosopher took it) to illustrate the inadequacy of defining man as a 'rational being': 'rational parrots' also exist. But the significance of the tale may lie in the fact that the bird in question addressed the prince in 'Brazilian', a 'language' the prince did not understand.

My guess is that its talents resembled those of Ya Lur. The anthropologist and born-again shaman Martin Prechtel recalls how, having observed the efforts of the Seventh-Day Adventists to convert the Mayan villagers, this true Polly-glot derailed their plans. The occasion was the arrival of 'two white-shirted, Bible-toting, soul-hunting, gigantic young missionaries':

Before either of them could manage to get a word out, Ya Lur oozed a loud, perfectly drawled west Texas 'Ha, haow or yeeoo?' Then without so much as a break to let it sink in that this was a bird speaking, she proceeded to deliver, to their drop-jawed amazement, a comical, spirited rendition of one of the missionaries' own hackneyed sermons in the worst imaginable bad Oklahoma-accented Mayan.

Ya Lur's genius for speaking in tongues upstaged the whites. In the village it was believed she could channel messages from the gods.

Prechtel offers a clue: 'Ya Lur was famous far and wide, and highly coveted by the villagers for the astounding fact that, unlike most parrots, she was trilingual and had a memory like a recording machine.' Her role was 'secretarial answering machine or voice mail' in the compound. But she always played back what she had been told with interest, her message being 'mixed in with playbacks of women walking past our compound arguing about the price of tomatoes, complaining about their neighbours'. On top of 'repeating any gossip whatsoever . . . redoing the dialogue using different silly parrot voices for each person', she would 'even imitate our laughter during her fine performances, repeating in turn even what we said about that. She was an auditory mirror.' No wonder that the villagers regarded 'a Lur speech as meaningful, mysterious, and coming from the world of the Deities'.[17] Like the shared mind of Brisbane's radio audience, hanging on Fritz's every utterance, the collective self-consciousness of the Tzutujil Mayan people of Santiago Atitlan is thoroughly mediatized.

The pathos of Léger's cockatoo is technological. Parrot is a memory system, which the inventions of Edison, Bell and

primero dia / perro — segundo dia / mona — tercero dia / isola — quarto dia / cana — quinto dia / tigure

Lumière superseded. Parrots contrive to imitate telephone bells; they cheerily catch the hiss and click of the phonograph needle; they learn to double the look of the mirror. But in the moving film they are museum pieces – even if, in a rearguard action, the Vadodara rickshaw driver and parrot trainer Amin Khan Pathan is teaching his parrots how to handle a camera, a trick that he calls 'cinema shooting'.[18] The individualistic Locke came upon his parrot story too late to realize what it signified. Humboldt stumbled upon his Indian-speaking parrots too early. Neither appreciated that, whether they alighted from the future or the past, the news that parrots brought concerned the media. Mediums themselves, they were their own message. Parrot, they teach us, is to be taken as we find it – like society.

The sacred calendar known as the Bourbon Codex was compiled by Aztec priests in the mid-17th century. This panel shows ten of the twenty named days in the 260-day almanac year.

ONLY AN EGG

As they grow older, the larger parrots are said to become 'venerable'. But it is our nostalgia for old things that makes us think them wise. In the preservation of the auditory patter of bygone ages, we recognize flea-market habitués like ourselves. Kakatua and Psittacus rarely distil their experience into any memorable apothegm. The fruit of their reflection tends to be a cynical cackle, imitative perhaps of the ancient noise they carry in their heads. When a still-lamented budgerigar, Sparkie Williams, fell off his perch, he prefaced his exit with these words addressed to Mrs Williams: 'I love you, mama.'[19] This wasn't bad considering that, in his heyday, Sparkie 'managed to master 583 words, including eight nursery rhymes, which he learned line by line',[20] and suggested that he intended to convey a sentiment. It also showed that Sparkie was all too human: instead of attaining a Buddha-like detachment, in old age he reverted to childhood. But perhaps I malign him. If, as a well-read budgie, he remembered his literary predecessor in Ovid, who, 'though dying . . . could still find utterance' ('And the last words he ever spoke were; "Corinna, farewell!"'),[21] he would have been alive to the fact that even parrot-dying has its rhetorical conventions.

If talking parrots give themselves away, it follows that the birds best fitted to be society's philosopher guardians will be silent or dead (or both). This certainly seems to be the case.

Parrot as pattern: woven silk, 6th century AD (perhaps Egyptian?).

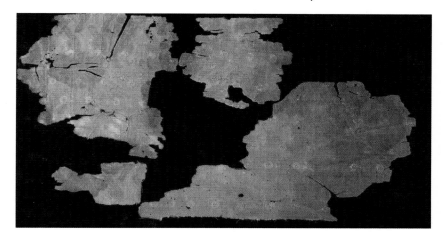

Voltaire's 'The Black and the White' ends in the following manner. Topaz undertakes to entertain Rustan with his parrot: 'He was born some time before the deluge; he has been in the ark; he has seen a great deal; yet he is but a year and a half old. He will relate to you his history, which is extremely interesting.' Rustan is enthusiastic and, 'The parrot being brought to him, spoke in this manner.'[22] But here the story ends, since it seems that the commonplace book in which the parrot's history was preserved has been misplaced. As regards the Flood, according to Boccaccio, the sole survivors, Deucalion and Pyrrha, had a son called Psittacus who 'when he had grown old, was transformed by the gods, at his own request, into a parrot'.[23] It's another reason for suspecting parrot is a Piscean.

The general rule is that the older the parrot the less it feels obliged to explain itself. Age difference is what counts, as Alice learns from the Australian lory in *Alice in Wonderland*:

> It has a long argument with her and finally grows sulky, saying "I'm older than you, and must know better." Alice doesn't accept this reasoning, but the lory refuses to tell its age, so the argument dwindles away.[24]

That's the point, for all their loquaciousness, parrots are masters of saying nothing. They know where to end, which is why authors find them so congenial. The apotheosis of parrot occurs in Flaubert's *Un Coeur simple*, where the elderly Félicité comes to confuse Loulou with the Paraclete, source of the gift of tongues – but not before her pet has died and been stuffed. In his stylistically polymorphic tour de force, *Flaubert's Parrot*, Julian Barnes draws attention to another parrot, mentioned in Flaubert's *L'Education sentimentale*. A man wandering through the wreckage of Paris after the 1848 uprising comes across a house that has remained

'Amazone' by name, Amazon by nature: like fiction, Flaubert's parrot is all that survives of the jungle of experience.

untouched. He sees through the window a clock, some prints hanging on a wall, and a bare parrot's perch. 'No parrot remained to tell the story of the carnage it had witnessed.'[25]

If we proceed backwards towards the Society parrot's infancy, we find it consistently associated with women. Gendered in this way, the female Polly is a patriarchal invention. The association patronizes women, although it captures aspects of their social and historical captivity. It also underestimates parrot. Sacheverell Sitwell compares the gaudily attired, but sententiously conservative parrot to 'Old dowagers dressed in crimped

satin/ Boxed in their rooms/ Like specimens beneath a glass/
Inviolate – and never changing,/ Their memory of emotions
dead.'[26] Presided over by 'a fine Mexican parrot',[27] the spinster
ladies in Virginia Woolf's *Jacob's Room* are more animated, but
all they can manage is small talk, opinions parroted without
conviction. An anonymous verse asserts that women are 'all of
them doves to the age of fifteen,/ Then wanton as sparrows till
forty they've seen;/ Then chatter like parrots till turned of three-
score.'[28] In *The Epicene* Ben Jonson characterizes the parrot as a
learned blue stocking. She is one of the perils Morose must confront if he marries: 'If learned, there was never such a parrot; all

your patrimony will be too little for the guests that must be invited to hear her speak Latin and Greek; and you must lie with her in those languages too, if you will please her.'[29]

It is women alone, though, who chiefly identify with caged parrots. Perhaps because they are usually waiting for men, they tend to be younger. The Chevalier de Boufflers, governor of Senegal from 1785 to 1787, liked to send his lover, the Comtesse de Sabran, parrots. After seven of them died in a single day, the exasperated countess drew two conclusions: she was out of love, and wished to be free.[30] Variations on this trope can, I expect, be found in most written and oral literatures. They are particularly exquisite in Tang China, no doubt reflecting women's roles there. One woman poet, referring to the Long Mountains famous for providing the Chinese middle class with 'white' parrots, manages a pun on 'west of the Long' and the word for 'cage'. This allows her to paint a sadly bitter picture of her present position. She came to the Brocade City (and her lover), like the parrot, from the desert; but now he ignores her, she is figuratively returned to the desert – only, thrust there by her lover's decree, she is not merely deserted but confined to a cage.[31]

The folly of younger women, married or unmarried, is proverbial in eighteenth-century English and French male literature. A rough typol(l)ogy of female parrots would include the social climber who, under stress, discloses her vulgar origins, swearing like a trooper (or parrot), and the sentimental girl so narcissistic that she falls in love with her mirror or parrot-self.[32] Jonathan Swift's women who 'only know the gross Desire' are hybrids of these types: 'Their Passions move in lower Spheres,/ Where-e'er Caprice of folly steers./ A Dog, a Parrot or an Ape . . . Engross the Fancies of the Fair.'[33] There is also the femme fatale, who shows off her fine feathers but is incapable of true affection, and the plausible charmer whose conversation proves on closer acquaintance to be time-wasting chatter – types blended a century later in William Wordsworth's condescending portrait of a parrot belonging to Mrs Luff (living at Fox-Ghyll in the Lake District) as 'a dazzling Belle,/ A Parrot of that famous kind/ Whose name is NON-PAREIL . . . [an] Arch, volatile, a sportive bird/ By social glee inspired;/ Ambitious to be seen and heard,/ And pleased to be admired.'[34] Addressing his sister, Wordsworth contrasted this flirtatious 'bird of the saloon/ By lady-fingers tended' with the 'darling' wren. But this preference is as conventional as the misogyny that informs it. Society's true parrot in this poem is none other than the poet himself.

Women writers have understood the relationship between women, parrots and society more intelligently. Eliza Haywood published two periodicals called *The Parrot*. The first, in the 1730s, contained her anti-Walpole writings; the second, published in the aftermath of the 1745 rebellion, tried to capitalize on the continuing preoccupation with the Young Pretender. Despite this she claimed that she 'never wrote anything in a political way'. Far from displaying a becoming female modesty, Haywood may have meant to express her view that the 'political' was defined far too narrowly: for women, politics was not confined to the parliament and the coffee-house. 'Self-consciously "parroting" information about trials, executions and appointments – information she reasonably could have collected and digested from other publications',[35] Haywood intelligently mimicked the generic diversity of the print media, whose proliferating discourses, hollow, conventional and shocking, increasingly supplied the mirror in which society identified itself.

Parrot's insider/outsider status, mocking but mocked, mirrors the terms in which emancipation presents itself to the self-aware woman. The green and yellow parrot in the opening line of Kate Chopin's *The Awakening* (probably a Yellow-naped

Double vision: the African grey looks at what the artist sees and at us looking at both. Beate Schaefer, *At the Window*, 2002, monotype.

Amazon, though the makers of the film *Grand Isle* chose a macaw) imitates what it hears. It 'speaks the language of the cosmopolitan New Orleans visitors who reside at Grand Isle in the summers'. It also speaks Spanish and French and English – and 'a language which nobody understood'. Perhaps it was

'Brazilian'. If the parrot represents Edna before awakening, it also hints at the need to discover an authentic pattern of speaking and behaving. Perhaps this is also indicated by its repetition (in French) of the phrase 'Go away, for God's sake'.[36] In feminist readings, the family pet changes its colours, signifying independence. At the end of *Now, Voyager*, the heroine (played by Bette Davis) famously refuses her male lover. Earlier she has predicted: 'I shall get a cat and a parrot and live alone in single blessedness.'[37] In this environment, parrot mocks the patriarchal preoccupation with genealogy – which, as we have seen, means relating *her*story differently. Thus Mondrian, the parrot in Ursule Molinaro's *Green Lights are Blue: A Pornosophic Novel* (1967), warns: 'It might be a mistake to turn backward, to dig up one's roots. Which might turn out to be unbearable when bared.' Heeding parrot's advice ('I was only an egg'), the novel proceeds parrot-wise, chapters 1–9 leading to chapters –9 to –1, and so back to chapter zero, the egg again.[38]

BUDGIE SMUGGLING

In the green and amorous youth of our species, parrots serve as a kind of avian Viagra. In the wild, as it were, parrot love is tame, durable and not without pathos: 'Pair bonding is very strong. Young parrots may choose their lifetime partners before maturity. In some of the species it is even possible that a bird will die after the loss of its mate.'[39] Parrot often understudies the role Shakespeare assigns to the dove. The two species may even marry: 'They lived in complete agreement,/ Their bond of faith held firm to the end./ What Pylades was to Orestes of Argos, that, Parrot, Turtle-dove was to you – while Fate allowed.'[40] Thus Ovid, painting a picture of humble hospitality, good cheer and endearing absent-mindedness: for without his devoted dove to care for him, what would 'that unaggressive creature,/ That talkative devotee of peace', parrot, have done, whose 'love of conversation/ Left him little leisure for food'?[41] In China and India, as well as Europe, parrot has been associated with ideas of intimacy, sociability and the arts of living together. This reputation depends, though, on generations of close observation of what it does in our zoos, aviaries and parlours. The fact is, as J. M. Forshaw points out, that 'Most of what is known about the breeding habits of parrots comes from captive birds.'[42] When it comes to imagining what parrots do when the cover is drawn over their cages at night, we rely mainly on what we fancy goes on in the human cage.

The Memoirs of the Swedish Academy for 1748 reported that a parrot 'which had been barren a long time, lay an egg without the coition of the male, merely from the sensation of a male of her own kind brought to some place'.[43] Perhaps it is this erotic susceptibility that explains why the Polyamory group, which promotes 'loving multiple people simultaneously', has adopted the parrot as its mascot. A Canadian polyamorist organizing a casual get-together brings along a stuffed parrot to help break the ice. Another explains, apologetically, that the great advantage of the parrot as a symbol is that it is humorous, 'a needed quality in such a staid, conservative group'.[44] The polyamorist's preferred species are the Scarlet macaw and the Cockatiel. The *Kama Sutra* advises women seeking a lover to cultivate:

Compared with the Mohini, this suka is like a *borogove*, thin and bedraggled (Cakresvara Temple, near Bombay, late 11th century).

> Solving riddles, enigmas, oral puzzles with hidden meaning; reciting verses beginning with the last letter of the verse recited by another person; inventing tongue-twisting phrases, their meanings distorted when uttered quickly; reading, including chanting and intonation; knowledge of stories, dramas, and legends . . . memorising literary passages and verses; repeating unfamiliar literary works by reading or hearing them once only . . . [45]

These are all skills that in one place or another are attributed to parrots.

The *Kama Sutra* also advises that when, under a battery of blows, sexual congress nears its conclusion, sounds like those of 'the dove, the cuckoo, the green pigeon, the parrot' may be made.[46] Silva reports that some parrots imitate humans. In macaws, 'treading is from the side. Female macaws will emit grunting sounds during the act. These carry some distance . . .' As for beating, the Palm cockatoo strikes the nesting site with a branch firmly held in its claws.[47] Anyone whose wardrobe of sexy underwear includes a parrot pouch will not fail to infer the Freudian meaning of this. The author of *My Secret Life* received his first sexual education at the hands (as it were) of a servant, memorable because 'Her lower lip was like a cherry, having a distinct cut down the middle, caused she said by the bite of a parrot, which nearly severed her lip when a girl.'[48] The beak as phallus: no doubt this explains the frisson the aforementioned Australian girls feel in pushing a finger through the wires. Such is the mingling of sexual parts, though, that the parrot penis is characteristically soft and cuddly. The parrot poucher may imagine fellatio, but he is lucky if he gets a nibble. *Budgie smugglers* are not agents of an illicit parrot trade: they are, in Australian slang, tight male swimming briefs that show off the genitals. Huddled in their pocket, the parts are imagined blindly

Gustave Courbet, *Woman with a Parrot*, 1866. Flying to her hand, the parrot makes the viewer's gaze mere *parrotry* of its desire.

bumping against one another like budgies in a bag.

In the thirteenth-century troubadour Arnaut de Carcassés' *Novas del papagai* (Tale of the Parrot), the parrot Pandarus visits a courtly lady with the news that Antiphanor, the king's son, is dying of lovesickness (which she alone can cure). Love has no use for oaths; love your husband publicly, and the prince secretly; Parrot's arguments are less persuasive than the eloquence with which he presents them. Meanwhile back with the prince, the parrot, a veritable cunning linguist, talks up the beauty of the lady, besides indulging in some flattering self-flattery ('My lord, no one/ will ever raise a parrot/ who will speak as well for his master's/ as I have done').[49] Parrot isn't simply a go-between. He creates the communication he pretends to report: without his amorous casuistry neither party would be engaged. It is not the desire of lady or prince that precipitates their affair, but Eros, whose sole aim in life is to create connections. Arnaut's parrot is polytelephonic: to draw eyes away from the adulterous lovers in the garden, it sets off alarm bells elsewhere, starting a fire in a nearby belfry.

COMPOUND GHOSTS

Artists may be particularly receptive to childhood's parrots. Recalling some of the experiences that contributed to his *psittacophilia*, Joseph Cornell singles out

> magic windows of yesterday . . . pet shop windows splashed with white tropical plumage . . . the kind of revelation symptomatic of city wanderings in another era . . . scintillating songs of Rossini and Bellini and the whole golden era of bel canto . . . indelible childhood memories of an old German woman a neighbour's pet parrot [*sic*] . . .[50]

Max Ernst's initiation seems to have been more traumatic. In 1906, when he was 14, Hornebom ('a multicoloured parrot, both intelligent and loyal') died on the same night that a sixth child was born into the family. This produced 'A sort of delirium of interpretation – as though the new little sister, Apollonia, born in all innocence at the very same moment, had taken to herself the zest for life, the vital energy, of his beloved bird.'[51] There followed 'a dangerous confusion between men and birds . . . and a tendency to identify himself with a bird of a higher species'. The parrot 'had to some extent become his totem'.[52]

A collective totem, whose cult some will find childish, is furnished by the popinjay. Edith Sitwell knew him as a type of vanity or empty conceit – 'Came the great Popinjay/ Smelling his nosegay:/ In cages like grots,/ The bird sang gavottes.'[53] At least he had the wit to rhyme on his own name. It is supposed that crossbow units in the later Crusades adopted parrots (encountered in the Near East) as their mascots or heraldic devices. In Germany, they called themselves Papageiengilde, and the head of the guild became known as the Parrot King. These guilds, the predecessors of today's shooting clubs, doubled as citizens' defence corps. They organized fairs featuring crossbow shooting

'Shooting the Popinjay', an 18th-century German woodcut.

at the wooden effigy of a parrot mounted on the top of a post. A parrot shooting fest, inaugurated by the Graf Count von Hoya in 1581, still survives in Hanover. Obviously, there was more to this than met the eye. As a mascot, the popinjay had a Masonic function, signifying membership of a secret society, an association remotely echoed in *The Magic Flute*. As a sign of valorous military service, it features in heraldic devices. The crest of the Sutton and Cheam Borough Council improbably boasts 'a popinjay proper gorged Gules holding in the dexter claw a Cross formy fitchy Sable'. Elsewhere, its image signifies 'Distinguished service in tropical countries'.

Psittacine heraldic devices.

Tracking back to the childhood of our kind, one finds the identification with parrots almost universal. A field guide to the polymorphic types inhabiting folklore, jokes, mythology and children's literature would be an encyclopaedia. If any generalization can be risked, it is that the appeal of the parrots who perch, crawl, cackle and mock their way through this forest of fiction mainly depends on the inversion of parrot and human characteristics: as parrots grow more human, the humans in these parrot tales grow more parrot-like. Parrots teach us the humanity we lacked. The anxiety this paradox can cause is illustrated by two early Victorian entries in *Blackwood's Magazine*. They relate, appropriately enough, to the education of children. Schoolboys, who are unintelligent mimics, one correspondent writes, are referred to as 'young *psittaci*', a rendering that captures the sound of their lisping chatter.[54] A year later parrots are no less disparagingly associated with an antithetical system of pedagogy – Pestalozzi's, which, giving full rein to the child's imitative habits, dispenses entirely with rules. In the acquisition of languages the result is 'an open violation of all the concords, and a general disregard of syntax'. Of Spanish and Italian, this critic claims, all the children 'ever acquired of their languages were such oaths and *mauvais mots* as

parrots pick up from sailors aboard ship, which they repeated
with all the innocence of parrots'.[55]

In the first case, parrots exhibit an excessive parity – as
Michel de Montaigne complains of pedants,

> We all know how to say: 'Cicero says thus; such are the
> morals of Plato; these are the very words of Aristotle.' But
> what do we say ourselves? What do we judge? What do
> we do? A Parrot could well say as much.[56]

In the second case, parrots indulge an embarrassing *disparity* – the source of endless jokes. Can the paradox be resolved?
Perhaps (with Plato in mind) the case of Aristodemus is to the
point: the type of the 'philosophical parrot who . . . really understands nothing', he copied Socrates' personal mannerisms but
not the principles of his thought.[57] Too alike to be truly alike, he
merely magnified the difference between understanding and
not understanding.

NOW YOU TELL ONE!

Passing the time –
'Now *you* tell one'
(from a 1930s
Scottish calendar).

Disparity jokes are the staple of parrot humour. Invariably, parrot repeats what it has heard out of place, with comic results. A catalogue of parrot tales collected in Indiana in the 1960s included such archetypal types as 'The Praying Parrots' (in which the 'I'm a whore' parrot is put in a cage with two religious parrots, in the hope that they will teach it to repent of its sins, but instead they cry out 'Our prayers are answered'); 'I'd Fall' (in which the purchaser of a singing parrot pulls one leg after the other and elicits a song, but, when he asks 'what happens if you pull both ribbons', receives the answer 'I'd fall on my ass'); 'How's Your' in which the parrot with one refrain ('How's your ass?') survives a sinking ship and asking his question one more time, elicits from a lady 'Aw, shut up!' 'And he says, 'So's mine, must be the salt water'; 'The Parrot and the Owl'; 'The Breeze'; 'The Parrot and the Bald Man'; 'Slit Throat Parrot'; 'The Parrot on the Truck'... And so on. 'The Parrot at the Foot of the Stairs.'[58]

In every case, the joke turns on the fact that the parrot is not a parrot at all: it doesn't parrot human phrases, but understands perfectly what they mean. The joke is: men speak and act thoughtlessly like parrots, but parrots possess a rational wit that is human. 'The Parrot at the Foot of the Stairs' joke (parrot, catching sight of his mistress's genitals, adapts a line from a popular TV commercial, squawking: 'How are you fixed for blades?') reveals something more; that parrots not only spike reason but give voice to our unspoken wishes.

The fullest and most fatal identification with parrot occurs in the Punchkin fairy tale. I referred to it earlier but, parrot-fashion, broke off. So, parrot-fashion, let's return to it here. It exists in many versions. In the Hindu version the seven daughters of a rajah, with their husbands, are transformed into stone by the great magician Punchkin, all save the youngest, whom Punchkin keeps shut up in a tower until by threats or coaxing he may prevail upon her to marry him. The captive princess leaves a son at home in the cradle, who grows up to manhood, and after long and weary wanderings finds his mother shut up in Punchkin's tower. Here he extracts from the evil magician the following:

> Hundreds of thousands of miles away there lies a desolate country covered with thick jungle. In the midst of the jungle grows a circle of palm-trees, and in the centre of the

circle stand six jars full of water, piled one above another; below the sixth jar is a small cage which contains a little green parrot; on the life of the parrot depends my life, and if the parrot is killed I must die.[59]

Of course, the young prince overcomes all the obstacles, retrieves the parrot, returns to Punchkin and successfully demands the release of his mother. Then, 'he proceeds to pull the parrot to pieces. As the wings and legs come away, so tumble off the arms and legs of the magician; and finally as the prince wrings the bird's neck, Punchkin twists his own head round and dies.'[60]

J. G. Frazer relates this story as an example of 'the doctrine of the external soul'; it would presuppose the 'Savage belief that animals, like men, are endowed with immortal souls'[61] – the idea presumably expressed by the Bororo when they told von Steinem that they were parrots. Out-of-body experiences characterize a number of nominally different folk tales – and they don't all end in parrot's dismemberment. In one variant, 'The brothers who are separated', the mother of two boys is turned into a parrot by a jealous rival. She aids them and is changed back to human form when they become successful. The human may become a parrot and be unable to return to his human form because of some trickery, as in 'The king transfers his soul to a parrot', a tale found also in Turkey, Turkestan and Mongolia. Two motifs deal with the parrot as a transformed human: 'transformation, man to parrot' and 'separable soul in parrot'.[62] The wise human-parrot may act as a spy for the master, guarding the wife, as in the parrot-mynah sequence.[63] The brave young shah of yet another version enjoys the best of both worlds. Changed into a parrot, he flies over the mountains and kidnaps Gala, a beautiful princess imprisoned by her father in a giant pomegranate. Mission accomplished, they wed. 'From that day all the parrots in the Shah's kingdom were treated with great respect. A parrot was even included in the royal coat-of-arms and fluttered from the army's banners, while to all the people it was a sacred symbol.'[64]

Perhaps these fairy tales are less childish than we thought. 'To a teacher of languages', Joseph Conrad reflects, in the Prologue to *Under Western Eyes*, 'there comes a time when the world is but a place of many words and man appears a mere talking animal not much more wonderful than a parrot'.[65] But perhaps that is wonderful enough. Recent research by Erich Jarvis permits us to speculate that human speech originates in a mimetic disposition. Studying the ability of hummingbirds, parrots and songbirds to learn songs, Jarvis finds this ability resides in the evolutionary specialization of a family of genes, glutamate receptors and their expression in the brain. His research predicts 'that the human language areas, too, may have specialized expression in these glutamate receptors, and if they do, you can use glutamate receptors to identify potentially the entire system of human language areas'.[66]

MISERY INDEX

The motives of parrot infantilization can be scientific, psychological or sycophantic (with an emphasis on the 'sick'). The phenomenon of 'delayed echolalia', often observed in autistic children, is colloquially called 'parrot speech'. It is surmised that it may be due to an 'inability to extract units of meaning from rapid streams of speech'. Articulateness is the result of disciplining an excess of communicativeness; babble has to be cut up into meaningful units before it can resemble speech. In the recent film *Paulie*, this logic is turned on its head: the

Looking at Looking: exhibited at the Paris Salon in 1868, Edouard Manet's *Woman with Parrot* is said to be an ironic comment on the artist's *Olympia* (1865). But it also alludes to Courbet's nude exhibited two years earlier (see p. 86). The model is Victorine Meurent.

eponymous bird (a Blue-crowned conure) helps his owner, 'a little girl with a debilitating stutter', to overcome her problem. Like parrots, people with special needs hold up a mirror to the shallow conventionality of our behaviour. Defending the value of mental heterogeneity, one Dr Rutkowski cites Mozart's bird-

Photographed in 2004, Mop the budgie from the Sunshine Coast of Australia 'could die at any moment because of the amount of energy he needs to fuel his huge feather growth'.

catcher, Papageno, as 'an archetype for humans with Down syndrome'. Papageno is endowed with the 'concrete intelligence' that children display: he knows what he does, why he does it; he knows his place, even if others don't – these are all characteristics of Down Syndrome. Further, Papageno displays an empathy for others that the more 'normal' characters lack. It is Papageno who revolts against the misogynistic order of Sarastro, and who recognizes the otherness of his namesake, Papagena.

But the people who work hardest to infantilize parrots are aviculturalists. Certainly, no other class of parrot-fanciers so curiously identifies the gratification of its own emotional needs with the best interests of parrot. Companion bird discourse is remarkable for its dependence on psychological jargon, an eclectic terminology derived from child psychology, clinical psychiatry and the popular literature of self-improvement. The chief motivation of aviculturalists is self-transformation. It is the cage of their own lives that they long to flee. And parrots are the chosen mode of transport. It follows that their well-being depends directly on the health and happiness of their pets. Much of the electronic chatter about parrot-keeping turns on sickness, on the identification of symptoms, their treatment and cure. Although they can communicate much else, parrots, it seems, cannot say what is wrong with them.

As the avian biologist James Murphy explains, the 'multibillion dollar worldwide companion bird business that has captured [sic] the hearts and minds of millions of people across the globe' is not about conservation. It is a one-way journey from jungle to 'Living Room'. The logical thing, then, is to select your breeding stock for its new role. 'Companion parrots', he explains, 'genetically selected for Health and Vigour, Natural Tameness and the Pronounced Ability to Talk not only reduce the stress on the parrots themselves but also provide the human household with a much more suitable companion.' 'Natural tameness' is critical. It is a 'juvenile trait' and is 'the key that unlocks domestication and a central ingredient in lowering the Misery Index of Parrots'.[67] The moral is clear: the happy parrot is the one who remains a juvenile throughout his life, a trait referred to as neoteny. Neotenized, he remains docile, placid, easily amused, playful and pliable. Parrot owners who want to exploit their pet's Pronounced Ability to Talk and keep him happy are advised to talk to him as if he were a baby.

Parrot owners don't want a parrot: they seek a companion. To this end, 'People raising baby parrots must become surrogate parents.' Interaction and attention shouldn't be confined to kisses and cuddles. 'Instructional interaction' is essential. Avoid 'punishment techniques' that are 'trust-destroying'. The benefits are many: 'my parrots often provide me with a much-

Legitimate above-shoulder parrots: Black-headed caique earrings by Patricia Golden.

needed attitude adjustment'. I find this pseudo-scientific language fascinating: what is the anxiety expressed in this desire to conceal affect? A dim sense of guilt attaches to the investment in parrot health. The fancier suspects that her parrot parenting substitutes for emotional failures in other parts of her life. One defensive tactic is to present these educational home truths as generally applicable. Correct training might be a model for the orderly, hierarchical organization of society as a whole: in any case 'One of the most significant mistakes people can make with their companion parrots is to allow them to run up their shoulder.'[68] Which no doubt explains the generally unreliable behaviour of pirates.

Talking to parrots is therapeutic for owners. At first 'people often do not know what to say to the bird'. The rules of parrot engagement follow those of human courtship: make sure you talk to, not at, parrot; remember: they 'are vain and love being praised or admired'. When initial contact has been established, venture on more intimate discourse: 'Name their little body parts and tell them how cute they are. Praise them for every little thing – whether they have consciously decided to be quiet while you were on the telephone, or if they just have pretty little black toes.' Don't be afraid of 'feeling particularly goofy' and if, despite this delightful solicitation of their interest, they ignore you, on no account abuse them as 'stupid'. Follow these protocols and the claim of parrot psychologist Chris Davis seems indisputable: while parrots have been profoundly altered to 'suit man's needs and considerable ego', 'Many [parrot-owners] are transformed, in some way, and don't know how, why, or when that transformation took place.'[69] The outsider suspects here a psychological and emotional *folie à deux*. An ersatz emotional economy substitutes for a realistic response to suffering. Conservation – not only the preservation of wild parrot habitat,

but a respect for inter-specific difference – is parroted back as 'conversation', an illusory communication based on the narcissistic fantasy that the other's desires must mirror one's own. This may prove that we can be parrots, but it provides no evidence that parrots are like us.

It also explains the saying 'sick as a parrot'. A parrot like Lewis Carroll's borogove ('a thin shabby-looking bird with its feathers sticking out all round')[70] simply won't be cheered up. Instead, he steadily mutilates himself. Self-plucking may be accompanied by a commentary: the 'Parrot Shrink' website suggests that owners monitor their sick birds' remarks as carefully as any doctor her patient's. A self-hatred for finery is indicated. Feathers furnish the plumes that write the texts – the verbal formulae, fixed in repetition, that the sociable fowl is condemned to imitate. Feathers are letters, and when it becomes plain that no amount of erudition can earn the parrot his freedom, he grows melancholy. He refuses to speak; he tears off his armature of feathery phrases, and stands naked and trembling.

Trade parrot: the macaw as Brazilian banknote, 1990s.

Flights of fancy are symptoms of caged-bird ownership. Putting the well-being of his parrots first, the parrot fancier acknowledges the sickness in his life he cannot fix.

A financial adviser recently stole more than 2 million pounds, which he used to build twenty aviaries in his garden with heating and running water to house his rare birds. He initially spent 450,000 pounds on the collection, which included palm cockatoos at 20,000 pounds a pair, Pesquet's parrots at 15,000 pounds a pair and Gang-gang cockatoos at 25,000 pounds a pair, then needed more money to feed them. He said he bought the birds for respite when his wife became depressed and his father was diagnosed with cancer.[71]

Letting the feathers grow back seems an obvious first step in restoring a parrot to health. Yet this, it seems, only makes the parrot-person more anxious. To assert his authority the replum-aged polly has to be trained: 'a bird with full wings and no training [is likely to] become a lost bird'. 'Most people who have trained a flighted bird say there is no going back.' But there is: the universe of the aviculturalist is like Kafka's Cathay – the parrot who succeeds in escaping from one cage simply finds herself inside another. For, of course, the wise trainer teaches her emancipated subject to fly to her mistress. No wonder that the trainer Chris Biro can reassure readers: free flying birds may enjoy greater 'mental fitness', but 'the greatest benefit of free flight is how it forces one to become a better bird trainer'.[72] As for the birds unfitted to belong to the new, purified avian society, what is their fate? What does 'Bye bye' mean to them? Too artificial to be released into the wild, they can 'live out their lives in open and unstressed surroundings'. But there are disturbing stories of 'desperate owners' and 'nearly naked frustrated bird[s]'.[73]

CRACKERS

A lady, exasperated by her parrot's obscene toilet humour, slit his throat. She took him out in the garden and dug a very nice, neat hole for him and laid him down in the grave on his back. She was standing over him and crying and sobbing that she wished he would come back and she was very, very sorry, when he looked up [between her legs] and said: 'Lady, if you can survive a crack like that, I can live forever.'[74] Buffon thought a sense of humour was confined to humans: so far as parrots go, the exact opposite may be true – parrots, I think, *only joke.*

A five-year-old Sun conure who 'often goes into a trance when we talk to her' 'is exhibiting her personal version of courtship display'. Macaws in a similar situation 'may fix their stare, contract their pupils and lean forward, usually with a vocal utterance they have learned such as "Hi!"'[75] 'Talk cures' are as commonplace in the caged-bird community as they are in the psychoanalyst's consulting room. Apropos of which: it is odd that the origins of Freud's leading ideas are parrotic. 'The talk therapies were essentially invented by Sigmund Freud, or, perhaps a little more historically honestly, by a woman called Anna O. Her real name was Bertha Pappenheim, and she was a patient of Freud's friend and colleague, Joseph Breuer.'[76] It seems that, in erasing 'Pappenheim' (a term any Freudian dream analyst must interpret as 'home of parrot fathers'), Freud suppressed the origins of his own talk cure. Nor can I repress the thought that another submerged link was forgotten here, as Pappenheim is where the famous fossil of the ur-parrot Archaeopteryx was discovered. I wonder whether Bertha's 'hysteria' wasn't really another case of borrowed identity *à la* Bororo: 'She developed a

Mark Catesby's engravings are often compared with those of Edwards (see p. 26), but Catesby always places a representative plant with the species depicted. Still, this Cuban paradise parrot looks prepared and garnished for representation.

bad cough that proved to have no physical basis. She developed some speech difficulties, then became mute, and then began speaking only in English, rather than her usual German'[77] – symptoms widely paralleled in the parrot-companion literature.

Of Carl Rogers's client-centred therapy, one writer admits

The therapist listens to the client and 'reflects' back significant thoughts and feelings by saying back to the client what he heard them say. Some therapists do this in mechanical fashion, which makes them sound like parrots with a college degree . . . [78]

Eugene Linden tells the story of parrot psychologist (no joke), Layne Dicker:

> Dicker, who is also a comedy writer, will tell a joke, causing his wife, Sally, to laugh. Then Hobbes, his miniature macaw, will laugh; then his Amazon parrot, Chicken, will laugh; and then, says Dicker, after all the laughter has died own, Dusky, another of his birds, will say 'Hee . . . hee . . . hee' very slowly, causing Layne and Sally to crack up, and the whole thing will start again. [79]

Linden's anecdote illustrates with uncanny accuracy Freud's suggestion that the essence of laughter is to be found in the fact that 'we do not know what we are laughing at . . . ultimately to

Paradise Regained: in this embroidered Bible cover (1651–2) a Suka – both clasped and clasping – adds lustre to the setting of the holy word.

break out laughing one does not need anything or anybody at all'.[80] Parrots, it seems, specialize in the solitary laughter that borders on hysteria.

If there is a business that should use parrot as its emblem, it is the office of 'Lost and Found'. Parrots hint at loss in a way that suggests loss can be repaired. Perhaps this is the pathos of the biscuit manufacturer's parrot, depicted with a cracker in his claw. About to crack the cracker, he illustrates the paradox of consumption, for it is 'Crackers' himself he prepares to eat. In the Arkansas artist David Stewart's three-dimensional assemblage 'First National Parrot', the eponymous bird eyes a cracker from which someone (the artist?) has taken a bite. In the company of Stewart's nostalgically assembled childhood objects, this hints at a lost relation. Cracked in half, the humble cracker becomes a symbol of lost and found. But perhaps it takes a parrot to see this. It is essentially the same misplacement that Gary Larsen brilliantly exploits in his cartoon. While three crims (or cons?) discuss their new hideout ('455 Elm Street . . . Let's all say it together about a hundred times so there'll be no screw-ups'),[81] three caged parrots stare dumbly into space. It's a play on the old trope of the parrot's indiscretion: when the detectives arrive, the abandoned birds will, of course, repeat what they have heard. The parrots are detectives in disguise. They will crack the case of the disappearing thieves.

Nowadays cages come in the form of pagodas, gracefully arching arbours, modular units that you can add on to, or other variations on the basic six-sided cube. But, as one cage consultant observes, 'the aviary is just the start of the containment'.[82] Inside their barred domain, parrot purchasers are reminded, 'birds that stand on the same size perches for 50–60 years are really prone to carpal tunnel syndrome' – not to mention frantic boredom. Natural tree branches (excluding oak and cherry – both toxic) are

Inside-out:
cage as sign of
spaciousness,
Algiers Hotel,
Miami Beach,
Florida, 1953.

recommended as perches ('their design is perfect'); and the arrangement of swings, a mobile or two and toys should be undertaken with the same care you bring to the arrangement of your own furniture. The good cage interior designer makes everything 'flow from the swing'.[83] As for the furniture, a luxuriously furnished parrot villa may boast kladders, crazy, curly corkscrews, tuggable goofy links, a jungle talk jukebox and even a quick-to-assemble playground kit.[84] If cages aspire to be bijou residences, aviaries parody our institutions of confinement: the prudent parrot breeder encloses his parrots inside a double fence; the cockie who laboriously jemmies herself out of her cage finds herself inside another enclosure, a no man's land where the electric light bulbs are never turned off. She is also in a position to see that hers is one among many cages. Usually this reality is concealed from her because of *baffles* between the neighbouring cells. These are designed to keep the avian inhabitants 'visually isolated from one another'. But be careful: 'No one wants to have a sick and possibly dying bird hidden behind a baffle.'[85]

In patriarchal societies women are parrots. Their comments on confinement (and parrots) are correspondingly more profound. Take the conundrum that confronts Mary, the narrator, in Mrs Gaskell's 'The Cage at Cranford'. The difficulty of finding a gift acceptable to Miss Pole is a hard nut that, when cracked open, turns out to contain a kernel that modestly says all we have said here. First, it takes us to Paris where Mrs Gordon, replying to the perplexed Mary's letter, suggests a cage of 'the newest and most elegant description', adding that cages are 'so much better made in Paris than anywhere else'. Our narrator is dismayed: 'however pretty a cage might be, it was something for Miss Pole's own self, and not for her parrot, that I had intended to get'. It's a nice distinction, but one lost on Miss Pole, who blandly accepts the offering for her parrot – 'I dare say a French cage will be quite an ornament to the room.' The trouble is that this cage is *faux*, a con – as the aptly named Fanny observes, 'Please, ma'am . . . there's no bottom to the cage, and Polly would fly away.' There is no top either. But, in the absence of a name for it, Miss Pole sets about sewing a bottom for her 'French thing' ('alas! That my present should be called a "thing"').

But in Mrs Gaskell's society, it's men, not women, who possess the right to bestow names, and, where women are concerned, the object of their naming is always to recall woman to her sexual function. Enter Mr Hoggins who, seeing the women labouring over their 'present for Polly-Cockatoo' begins to laugh 'in his boisterous vulgar way'. 'For Polly – ha! ha! It's meant for you, Miss Pole – ha! ha! It's a *new invention* to hold your gowns out

– ha! ha!'. Miss Pole thinks this a dirty joke – quite rightly – but Mr Hoggins defends himself, showing the ladies an illustration of the thing in his wife's fashion-book. Not only is the women's inventiveness confined inside a signification of male invention; their ignorance of the thing's signification implies an innocence of their own function. As John Skelton remarks, 'In Popering grew peres, whan Parrot was an eg'.[86] A Poperin pear is a penis; it's also the parrot of the open cage. Miss Pole's hymeneal repair is too late; the egg has hatched, the joke bolted. But that's not quite all. Recovering themselves, as it were ('we were quite ourselves again'), the ladies counter their patriarchal capture and humiliation by improvising hoods ('two very comfortable English calashes')[87] for themselves. In Freudian terms, unnaming the cage, they find in 'the French thing' something that makes sense of their world.

By contrast, the Dead Parrot sketch, originally broadcast in the first series of *Monty Python's Flying Circus*, and so well known to British television viewers as to be part of their folk mythology, eschews an ending. The ex-parrot may have joined 'the bleedin' choir invisible' – become a 'thing' – but not the sketch, which the writers keep alive by offering readers/viewers alternative endings. In one the sergeant-major intervenes, and on the grounds that the sketch has become too silly, marches the customer off to do another sketch. In the second, the owner reveals his secret longing to be a lumberjack. In the third, the owner invites the customer back to his place. It's this last, weakest ending that I like best. It seems to be a non sequitur, a kind of abandonment of plot. As for its ludicrous anti-climax, the fact that it parrots a kind of Kenneth Williams radio innuendo, this merely identifies it as an authentic parrot production.

When we take account of the fact that parrots not only copy us but talk in a hoarse voice that is oddly their own, a different history of human engagement emerges, where parrots play a far more creative role. Instead of dipping out of sight into the jungle of the unconscious, they are discovered in flocks discreetly sipping at the corners of the great lake known as the Mirror of Language. Thence they bear away liquid syllables, and the ambition to crystallize these into words, articulate images of their own beauty. Isn't it the dilution of this pre-diluvial fullness of utterance that Apollinaire laments when, with reference to Scarlet macaws, as well as Paris, he writes: 'O Paris/ From red to green all the yellow dies '?[88] As rainbows, images of meeting places where we might truly meet, parrots suggest both the inaccessible and the vulnerable. Perhaps this is why, in the present-day icono-literature of disappearing habitats, parrots always seem to rocket across rivers and clearings.

We have been too much with visible parrots. Poetic parrots belong to the unseen. Poetic speech is driven by the same insight parrots display when 'out in the sunshine looking for a mate . . . she or he looks for one whose plumage fluoresces in the sun's ultraviolet light as an indicator of quality'.[89] In the best poetic/parrotic literature, parrots are visions. They are angelic messengers. Opening a place that could never be unilaterally named, caged and sold into slavery, parrots symbolize the inner gold that greed can never trade. 'The Smokers', wrote John Shaw Neilson, with reference to the Regent parrot, 'have washed in the sunlight/ And taken the gold.' And, because of the other-worldly nature of its communication, Neilson advised treading carefully, 'Gently they say he is not of the Earth, /He only falls below.'[90]

Flight from reality: compare this mutant Princess of Wales parakeet with Edward Lear's truly alchemical aristocrat on p. 127.

And our unwillingness to consider parrot speech on a par with our own means that, when parrots are not identified with angels, they are thought of as parasites. In the entertainment industry, their voices have not only come from below but from inside. A short history of ventriloquial parrots might begin with Joseph Askins's 'triumphant engagements at Sadler's Wells Theatre in London in 1796 and 1797'[91] and end with the American TV entertainer Terry Bennett's Sunday airing *Let's Have Fun* show, with its popular 'Peter Parrot' ('who tries to repeat everything you teach him')[92] segment. By 1967 commercialism had killed Bennett's parrot: in contrast, Askins's parrot, like Monty Python's Norwegian blue, was dead on arrival – after conducting a dialogue with a 'supposed parrot in his left coat pocket', he used to unfold a couple of handkerchiefs concealed in his lap to reveal nothing inside them (astonishing an audience 'whose senses had believed he really had a bird concealed in his pocket'). Either way, parrots were a minor species of the ventriloquist's doll family, and if, as has been suggested, throughout the Romantic period, attention remained on the ventriloquist rather than the doll, their role was not to originate but to echo. Perhaps their contribution to the art was mechanical rather than mimetic: Baron de Mengen, an early ventriloquial amateur, used a doll 'with a mouth like a kind of nutcracker'.[93]

In other cultures communication is less exclusively associated with the successful caging of the voice. The free flight of the tongue is encouraged. Imitativeness is understood actively. In contrast with the Genesis myth, which casts unfallen man and woman as God's ventriloquists, Meso-American cultures locate the invention of language in an onomatopoeic faculty. Speech arises out of cacophony, not silence. Oddly, it is that most articulate of poets, Wallace Stevens, who best communicates this insight to non-Spanish-speaking Americans. In his poem 'The Comedian as the Letter C', 'The affectionate emigrant found/ A new reality in parrot-squawks.'[94] The idea, that in the New World, meanings are generated onomatopoeically – *squawk* enacting sonically the meaning of the word – is a poetic item of faith among the Latin American Modernistas. In Manuel Angel Asturias's *Leyendas de Guatemala*, the narrator

> travels to the dense Guatemalan jungle and encounters his ancestors and their makers celebrating the original creation. A key moment in this 'delirious night' enacts the coming into being of primal sounds, song, and language out of the silent void that preceded them: 'In the darkness nothing exists. Grasping my one hand with the other, I dance to the rhythm of the vowels of a scream A-e-i-o-u!'[95]

This lost, pre-linguistic world is not speechless, enveloped in eerie silence. It is alive with the primary colours of language,

There are three species of Blue macaw from Brazil, the Hyacinthine, Glaucous and Lear's. London Zoo had specimens of all three as early as 1836.

clicks, squawks and whistles, the 'first scream of the flesh', a kind of all-speak.[96] How could this furnish meaningful speech? To answer this it's enough to glance at the character of Guacamayo in Asturias's highly experimental 'ethnographic play' *Cuculcan*, based on the *Popol Vuh* and the books of Chilam Balam. The play enacts a series of encounters between the

Pre-Columbian
Art Deco: book
cover, Paris, 1923.

supreme serpent-god Cuculcan and the Guacamayo, 'a verbal trickster embodied in a parrot of many colours'. These are said to embody two opposed theories of language and identity. Cuculcan's promotion of 'the power of an all-encompassing language sufficient to itself' opposes Guacamayo's advocacy of 'the duplicity and foreignness of language and its consequent critical power'. One is 'hostile to the intrusion of alien speech', the other, 'who as a parrot by definition speaks with quotation marks, that is, with the words of others, embodies the persistent foreignness of language'.

'As a diviner, a storyteller, and a verbal gymnast', the 'bird of enchantment' speaks in a 'jerigonza [gibberish] of colours', with words like lies 'clothed in precious stones'. The 'rainbow of his voice' emerges from the Guacamayo's feathers, like the 'rich plumage and perfect colour' of his words. And, unlike the light of reason, Guacamayo's 'voice of fire' has the power to excoriate the blandness of power. His 'incorrect' or deliberately misused words curl round the texts of power, his mocking tongues like flames reducing them to ashes. In the Guacamayo's presence 'Cuculcan's orderly journey through the days' is turned into 'a symphonic babble orchestrated by the poetic parrot's linguistic play' – as the stage directions indicate:

dog barks, chicken cacklings, tempest thunderclaps, serpent hissings, troupial, guardabarranca, *and mockingbird warblings, are heard as the Guacamayo names them, just as the cry of children, the laughter of women [give voice to] the commotion and chatter of a multitude that passes.*

Like Prechtel's Ya Lur, Guacamayo represents the voice of society. The noise he reproduces is the sound of the collective voice, democratic where Cuculcan's is dictatorial, multiple rather than one.

In Anton Reichenow's *Vogelbilder aus fernen Zonen* (Kassel, 1878–83), the artist Gustav Mützel experimented with a colour-based zoo-geography. All the members of this saffron-hued 'family' come from South America.

Above all, it is the voice of the meeting place. As the warrior Chinchibirin says, 'A market is like a Great Guacamayo, everybody talks, everybody offers coloured things, everybody deceives.'

If, after this, someone still wants to know what 'the pure word' is that stands at the threshold of language, the answer is

Taking possession: Piri Re'is's *Chart of the Ocean Sea* (Gallipoli, 1513) represents newly discovered Caribbean islands as parrot perches.

by now surely obvious. It's the parrot's own squawked *ca-ca* – Italian baby-talk for 'poo'. Only a Freudian would say this was shit. Ka may be the first word in Hindu mythology, but in the history of the New World, it is ca-ca, the ironic repetition of the sound, that signifies, the same sound parodied (parroted?) in Guacamayo's own name. Returning from his first Caribbean voyage in 1492, Columbus brought with him a pair of Cuban Amazons for his patron, Queen Isabella of Spain. Recalling this in his 1969 essay, 'America, la engañadora', and with the Popol Vuh's portrayal of the parrot as a colourful trickster in mind, Asturias suggests that this set the tone of future communication. Unable to resist cannons and swords, the Fourth World peoples defended themselves against the European invaders in the only way they could: by parroting back what was said to them.[97]

This suggests something else: that the Taino and other Caribbean peoples parroted back what the Europeans said because the latter behaved like parrots. As Gerald Sider comments, in treating the Taino as human parrots, ideally suited for enslavement and conversion, Columbus and his successors 'parrot[ed] their own fantasies of native intentionality'.[98] If my speculation, that such communication as occurred took the form of echoic mimicry improvised around the syllable 'ca' (hence canoe, cannibal, Caribbean, etc.),[99] then it seems that Wallace Stevens's Crispin was not far wrong: in future, history, as well as poetry, would be composed of 'parrot-squawks'.

FLOCK DYNAMIC

Against this background of cacophonous glee, the idea that parrots must be trained to talk seems self-interested. Evidently, what is at stake here is not expression as such but our desire to cultivate a kind of talk-talk answering to our own straitened idea of communication. The result of the bird's assimilation to our needs is an emotional dependence whose symptoms are an excessive empty chatter, an obsessive preoccupation with the cage's constructional principles (always looking for the key), and an intermittent melancholia captured in a preoccupied, faraway look. The social implications are profound. Inducted into isolation, the parrot's self-image is human: restored by chance to the company of other, similarly bred parrots, it keeps its own counsel. In the aviary of humanized parrots, the birds mumble to themselves, not recognizing their neighbours as parrots at all.

Anecdotes about talking parrots are everywhere. Perhaps for the same reason, they are highly repetitive. In an environment designed to eliminate surprise, repetition itself acquires significance. The mere fact of saying the same thing over and over seems to give life meaning. Sir Thomas Dick Lauder reports that when the Emperor Basilius Macedo imprisoned his son on the advice of jealous courtiers, his parrot kept up the

Science? Art? Imperialism? Only the parrot can say which imitates which in this engraving from Pierre Sonnerat's *Voyage à la Nouvelle Guinée* (Paris, 1776).

refrain 'Alas! Alas! Poor Prince Leo'. This being repeated pricked the conscience of the emperor's courtiers, and they confessed their disloyalty.[100] In the same vein, Roman Catholic congregations might be shamed into piety by a parrot word-perfect in the Mass.[101] Colonel O'Kelly's parrot, 'whose imitative talent was reckoned most extraordinary', made repetition an item of faith. It 'not only repeated a great number of sentences, and answered questions, but was able to whistle, with the greatest clearness and precision, the 104th Psalm, "The Banks of the Dee," "God save the King," and other favourite songs' – 'if by chance it mistook a note, it would revert to the bar where the mistake occurred, and finish the tune with great accuracy'.[102]

As a man-taught mimic, parrot's wit is measured by its skill in orchestrating repetition. Robbins relates an eighteenth-century fable

> In which the famished crew of a becalmed ship eats first the parakeets, then the cardinals and the cockatoos, and finally the overconfident parrot, which had been saying all along, mimicking the captain, that everything would turn out fine (and so chose not to escape through the hole in its cage).[103]

This parrot could have learnt a thing or two from Charlotte, King George v's African grey, who

> viewed State and confidential documents with a critical eye from her favourite perch on the King's shoulder, and [who] sometimes, when feeling that matters demanded active intervention, would call out in a strident seafaring voice, 'What about it?'[104]

Charlotte, like the transformed Bodhisattva, knew when to speak and when to hold her tongue.

Good timing is the difference between pardonable cheek and punishable stupidity. Did you hear the one about the man on the plane? He couldn't get his cup of coffee because, every time he asked, the parrot next to him squawked for another whisky. The parrot's abusive rudeness so flustered the stewardess that she repeatedly forgot the man's coffee. Finally, the man decided to imitate the parrot, and abused her. Next thing they knew, two burly stewards wrenched them from their seats and threw them out of the emergency exit. As they plunged earthwards, the parrot turned to the man and said: 'For someone who can't fly, you sure are a lippy bastard.'[105] The wise parrot not only knows how to forge repetition into the key of freedom. He also knows when and where to do it.

The bad press that philosophers give parrots reflects the environment in which parrots are supposed to learn. Locke, Descartes and Hume share Columbus's view that the mind of parrot is a blank slate, ready to be inscribed with instructions for slaves. If this is reasonable, any sign that parrot can think for itself is unreasonable. The story of Prince Maurice and the parrot left Locke philosophically dumbstruck. The archetypal parrot-talker is vociferous because it is empty-headed. In this regard it is the avian equivalent of the about-to-be-enslaved native – who, for the purposes of enslavement, must be assumed to have no will or culture of her own. Of course, the main effect of this is to lock the colonizer inside the cage of his own emotional infancy. It is no accident that in colonial Australia, Aboriginal men and women shared their white-imposed nicknames (respectively Jacky-Jacky and Polly) with parrots. I don't find it at all surprising that Robinson Crusoe's Polly fails to tell her master about the cannibals: to minister to his self-pity, she had forgotten the 'Brazilian' of her polyglot tribe and the ca-syllable whence the universe came. In her story 'The Parrot and Descartes' Pauline Melville's South American Amazon reflects on the limitations of her owner's logic: 'reason tells us reason has its limits, thought the parrot. And he was so delighted with his own wit, that he let out an involuntary laugh which had the servants searching all night for an intruder.'[106]

Laughter is the cacophonous supplement of speech. It is the dynamic discourse of the flock that the parrot forfeits when it is traded or bred for the silence of the cage. In this context, efforts to cheer up captive parrots are a kind of psychological ventriloquism. To make up for the sole parrot's 'instinctive delight in group interaction', one aviculturalist advises owners 'to include their parrot(s) in the more social human rituals, such as grooming/preening in the bathroom in the morning, and enjoying meals together. Much use can also be made of the visits from friends. 'Here', she adds, 'we take the opportunity provided by such visits to order pizza and this is shared by all, humans and parrots alike.'[107] Other, wilder identifications and doublings are entertained:

Bidding or for sale? Parrot as marketplace totem in *A Market Stall in East India* attributed to Albert Eckhout (1610–1666). The prominence of New World fruit suggests that the true exotic here is the parrot.

Parrots in the wild are playful and have even been observed to make snowballs and play with them. If we allow ourselves to become more playful, our parrots will respond happily and with appreciation of the exuberance and abandon such silliness can manifest. Physical play, such as tossing things back and forth, can also be appreciated. However, the majority of my parrots adore it most when we engage in mutual silliness. There is nothing my Amazon loves more than when I stand by his cage, calling him over dramatically saying, 'Come 'ere you! Come 'ere you sexy Amazon. Give me a kiss!!!'[108]

By such means we feather the nest of our lovelessness. But the cruelty we inflict when we deduct parrot from its flock leaves a scar. The ornateness of cages may sublimate the guilt we feel, as if richness of ornament can compensate for the loss of free flight amid jewel-like but living companions. These reflections gain a further ironic twist when the jailkeeper is herself imprisoned. Ma Shouzhen, one of the Four Talented Courtesans of Qinhuai (1548–1604), writes: 'All day long I watch the parrot/ Pass its life in a golden cage./ Emerald-plumed, it is skilled in brushing its feathers;/ Its vermilion beak is good at harmonising sounds', adding, 'By the mond trees the heart is wont to break'. Just as the poverty of parrot's inner life is disguised by the richness of its external gilding, so with the poet's empty heart: the fine clothes and jewels she wears conceal it. In these sessions of bittersweet solitude 'Pleasure never is at home'.[109] It's on the wing where, reunited with parrot's brothers, there is the freedom not to talk. As the caged *tuti* (parrot) in Jalaluddin Rumi's *Merchant and the Parrot* reflects wistfully to its master, 'I could risk a sweet exchange/ Of our positions. I would never make you sing/ But send you to your brothers . . . The silence could be beautiful . . . I could rediscover what a simple thing it is to fly.'[110]

In this connection the behaviour of Dr Urbino's vocally virtuosic 'royal Paramaribo' in Gabriel García Márquez's *Love in the Time of Cholera* is encouraging. When the President of the Republic wishes to confirm for himself the truth of his reputation, the parrot refuses for two hours to utter a single syllable, 'ignoring the pleas and threats of public humiliation of Dr Urbino'.[111] The bird knows a dictator when he sees one.

In the technical language of parrotology, 'flock dynamic' is the tendency of the human imagination to see the many in the one. It is this marketplace of colourful sound that is closed down when, in the fine and private place of the cage, parrots are taught to echo what Ma Shouzhen calls our 'boudoir feelings'.[112]

Like speaks to like, or Who's leading whom? William Lewis Herndon, *Exploration of the Valley of the Amazon*, 1854.

PIECES OF EIGHT

The parrot's power of repetition naturally appeals to storytellers. The great Italian folklorists Comparetti and Pitré both printed 'The Parrot' (a story that Italo Calvino retells in his *Italian Folktales*) 'at the beginning of their anthologies as a kind of prologue'. The parrot symbolizes the storyteller's art. The nature of that art is plain from the story itself, where the parrot's own interminable tale so distracts the girl that the bird successfully foils the designs of the lustful king. It is the simple deferral of an ending that prevents her fall. The moral is clear: virtue is better served by fairy tales than sermons. According to Calvino, the parrot qua storyteller's ability to cast a spell over the listener has a political as well as moral dimension. It suggests that common people can resist the will of the powerful, and through their tale-telling create alternative endings.[113] Perhaps I am too hard on the caged-bird crowd. Like the birds they capture, they pine for a lost community of voices, and, in the absence of storytellers prepared to repeat the old fairy tales,

seek consolation from what is next best, the sound of their own voices echoing old familiar sayings.

Variations on this role are perhaps infinite. As the benevolent daimon perched on the narrator's shoulder, parrots legitimize the desire to be set free. They are the geniuses of beginnings. In this role they not only provide the momentum of fairy tales: they furnish guides for real adventures. The Dyaks of Sarawak used to say to an explorer 'You are our parrot, we will follow you.'[114] In the same spirit, native American guides habitually carried a small parrot on their hand. But the best example of parrot as traveller's totem comes from the literature of Australian exploration. In the early 1840s Charles Sturt based his plan of inland exploration on the flightpaths of budgerigars or Shell parroquets:

> I had seen the *Psytacus Novae Hollandiae* and the Shell Parroquet following the line of the shore of St Vincent Gulf like flights of starlings in England . . . they all came from the north and followed in the same direction . . . a reasonable inference may be drawn from the regular and systematic migration of the feathered races.[115]

Here, parrots literally give the writer a sense of direction. Worthless as a scientific hypothesis, Sturt's budgies provided a plot, a reason for his narrative. Exactly the same role is played by Iago, the parrot in Hergé's *The Castafiore Diamond*. This, as Tintin buffs will recall, is famously the adventure where nothing happens. To maintain the supposition of a theft, Hergé introduces every kind of whodunit stereotype. Gypsies, paparazzi, the diva's accompanist – all have a motive, all (in the closed world of the detective story) signify suspicion. In the end there is no human culprit at all, only a magpie with a taste for lining its nests with jewels, its role identified when Madame

In *Parrots and Other Birds*, Frans Snyder (1579–1657) uses composition to camouflage a cabinet of curiosity collection as evidence of the wealth of the wild.

Castafiore stars in *La Gazza Ladra*. The genius of this tale of theft without a thief is Iago, the hybrid-plumaged macaw Madame has bestowed on her reluctant host, Captain Barnacle. Iago plays the role of telephone, doubling up live conversations, but he stands for the nature of the tale itself, which, as Michel Serres says, is a tale about noise – not just because it is filled with thumps, squawks, recorded music, rehearsed arias and importunately ringing telephones, but because the excess of communication produces a plot where nothing happens.[116]

As provocative repetiteurs, parrots start stories and keep them going. As the Monty Python sketch illustrates, they also deal with the problem of endings. They don't manage this by ingeniously tying up the loose ends. Quite the reverse, they do it by showing that the well-made ending is the door and lock of the narrative cage, and that the only emancipatory ending involves prizing it open. In David Levine's short story 'A Festival of Parrots', a story told by the children is appropriated by their father. The children

> had never thought of a suitable ending for the Festival of Parrots. We didn't know why the villagers celebrated it and what happened to all the parrots when they were done. It didn't matter. All that mattered was the night we'd invented it, the delicious joy in imagining together the screeching, maddened parrots and the feather-deluged village.[117]

But, incorporated into father's calendar, repeated annually at family gatherings, the tale has lost its joyous open-endedness. When, after one retelling, our narrator finally realizes how the story ends, he understands that it is the very idea of a plot, a masterful story-teller and a compliant subject matter that have to be rejected:

Black and white? One of seven species of Amazon macaw, the Blue and yellow macaw (*Ara ararauna*, Linnaeus, 1758) is distributed in rapidly dwindling numbers from the rain forests of Panama to northern Paraguay.

It seemed that in the last few hours the village children dressed up as parrots, as feathery and gaudy as the parrots themselves. They went running down the feather-strewn street, opening every cage and urging the parrots to fly free – while the birds, bald and scrawny, looked out and would not move.[118]

'In parrot lore, one of the most widespread stories is of a lost parrot that was returned to its owners when it said, "Hello, this is 557-3245. Please leave a message after the beep".'[119] For some reason this reminds me of another story: 'Eight cockatiels stolen from a British aviary have been tracked down after a person heard their trademark call – a whistled rendition of the Laurel and Hardy theme tune.' 'The cockatiels picked up the famous tune from a new arrival to the aviary', the owner said. 'That bird had previously been kept in an indoor cage and its owner had taught it to whistle the Laurel and Hardy', he said. 'When I brought it down here some of the other birds started to whistle as well.'[120] This seems to contradict the rule that parrots only exercise their imitative faculties in captivity, responding exclusively to human sounds. Or does it? Perhaps the Cockatiels only mimicked the newcomer because they mistook him for a human being.

These stories illustrate an interesting point about parrot repetition. Parrot repetitions are newsworthy when they occur in different places. In the same way, they are variously scandalous, absurd or poignant when repeated at the wrong time. As the telephone story shows, by repeating a phrase they can find what has been lost, bring back what has been scattered abroad. Parrot repetition, then, is a principle of association, a way of joining formerly distant things. The novelty of this is plain if we think of poetry: poets use metaphors when they want to establish a resemblance between formerly unrelated ideas or objects. The parrot achieves the same effect by cultivating an art of repetition *out of context*. It is by this means that parrot becomes the spokesperson of society, since scandal (the argot of social intercourse) is nothing other than items of hearsay and rumour repeated at the wrong time or place. And the beauty of these disreputable titbits is that they have no

The Princess of Wales parakeet painted by Edward Lear has many other names. It is found in the interior of Central and Western Australia. Lear knew it as the Roseate parrot.

Bird fancier: a jolly Persian lass and her amusing Polly by Lucien Mouillard, 1908.

source. When Casanova wanted revenge on a former mistress, he taught his parrot to denounce her virtue, then offered the bird for sale in a public place. The victim of his slander consulted her lawyer in vain – 'a parrot could not be indicted for libel'. In the end, the only way to shut the bird up is to buy him – for the outrageous price of 50 guineas. The rake's revenge is sweet and profitable.

Talking about Casanova brings to mind another case where the parrot's status as an eyewitness is in question. In Erle Stanley Gardner's *The Case of the Perjured Parrot*, Casanova (that's the name of the parrot) apparently identifies his master's murderer ('Helen, put down that gun!'). It turns out, though, that the parrot found at the scene of the crime is not Casanova, but a look-alike substitute, shortly thereafter 'brutally murdered'. This confusion of parrots and men is complete when, at the inquest, the district attorney announces: 'I want the words

Hopping about like a bird: Wallace Beery as Long John Silver in Victor Fleming's film of 1934, *Treasure Island.*

of this parrot on the record. The parrot is accusing the witness. I want the record to show it.' To which Perry Mason suavely responds: 'if the parrot is to be a witness I should have some right of cross-examination'. Parrot is an unreliable eyewitness – a whole play, 'The Stool Parrot' after a story by Damon Runyon, centres on efforts to persuade a murder-witness parrot to say, or not to say, what she saw – but its talent for seeing links between the strangest of things makes it the natural ally of the literary detective with his genius for deductive logic.

Repetition becomes in the human mind a form of syco-phancy, and those who repeat what is said to them are suspect-ed of bad faith. Doubles 'show a worrying lack of scruples about the fracture between their emotional investment and their insincere self-representations'.[121] Hypocrites and sycophants, doubles pose as sincere but easily give themselves away– wit-ness Martial's story of 'the man who paid a compliment to

Breeding ghosts: the first reports of this Budgerigar spangle grey dominant mutation came from Australia in 1978. A society dedicated to the mutation was founded in the UK in 1988.

Caesar by giving him a parrot which had been taught to say: "I, a parrot, am willing to learn the names of others from you. This I leant to say by myself – Hail Caesar".' (This parrot's 'Hail' [Ave] is really a self-address, since the Latin for bird is *avis*.)[122]

Parrots are parasites: in Rome, where parasites were professional guests employed to play the fool at dinner parties, this was literally the case. Sukas were plied with wine to make them speak more freely (in the eighteenth century the same method was used in teaching parrots to speak). Doubles are misers about money – a man bidding for a talking parrot is repeatedly outbid; when he eventually gets the parrot at a vastly inflated price, he asks his new pet: 'Can you really talk?' 'Of course', the bird answers, 'who do you think was bidding against you?' Doubles lack discretion: when they get what they secretly want, they boast about it, like the pious parrots that, when the 'I'm a whore' parrot is put in their cage for re-education, cry out instead 'Our prayers are answered.'

It is no accident that Robert Louis Stevenson's singular character, Long John Silver, has a parrot 'name[d] after the most ruthless and dreaded pirate on the high seas, of whom Silver is himself in some sense just the double or son'.[123] But, if doubles possess us, they can also be used to release us from another's possession. This seems to be the lesson of the ninth-century No play, 'Komachi's Parrot-Answer Poem', in which Ono Komachi employs a literary genre known as the *omugaeshi*, or parrot-answer ('When a reply to a poem is very much like the poem, then it is called a parrot-answer poem'),[124] to reply to a poem the Emperor has sent her. Taking the convention to an extreme, she changes only one word of the Emperor's poem. This, as the Emperor's servant observes, is either daring or foolhardy. Maybe it signifies Komachi's loss of creative power, her decline into the role of mere parrot. Or maybe it demonstrates her continuing mastery of the haiku form: the writer is the only servant who can re-master the master, and in aping him author her own difference.

PARA

The breeding programmes of aviculturalists across northern Europe and the UK have produced a shadow flock of mutant lories, cockatiels, budgerigars and macaws, and their concomitant spaces – hundreds of thousands of cages, wire-netting who knows how many cubic miles of air. Cheering up a cheerless landscape of backyards, garden sheds, allotments and garages, the relentlessly happy chatter of these refugees from the real world spills over into the neighbourhood, mingling with the flat roar of traffic. These pale and speckled mutants subliminally colonize the senses, bringing Australia, India and Africa into contact with our washing-lines and net curtains. But this environmental transformation is puny in comparison with the power of the media to amalgamate images into novel species of signification, and to cross-fertilize these to produce new flocks of association, useful in advertising, comic books, the naming of the newly discovered and, indeed, of whatever ironically brings into question the sovereignty of the simple, unequivocally factual.

Talking to friends about what I was doing, it soon became clear that 'parrot', the word, was breeding a flock of new conversations. Did I know about the remarkable Roy, invented by novelist Christopher Hope, who single-beakedly tested the South African apartheid system? Had I made room in my literary aviary for Enid Blyton's beloved Kiki, or Stevenson's aforementioned Captain Flint, or Aristotle, for Thomas Bernhard's Friedrich or Samuel Pepys's Pauline? What about Blossom who fainted when she saw death? Did I intend to discuss the extraordinary case of the maniacs frightened by parrots, or Jan Fabre's popinjays, or

John Oliver's Guacamayo Suite (performed in Toronto), not to mention the Kakadu Variations and the ur-fowl of Max Ernst?

John Skelton's parrot (he makes his appearance in a long satirical poem called *Speke Parott*, written around 1520 in London) is descended in the approved manner from Paradise ('My name is Parott, a byrde of Paradyse'), but its way of talking is decidedly un-Adam-like. Skelton's parrot shows (what Julian Barnes showed again more recently) that identity of voice and identity of style are unrelated. As Barnes parodies different storytelling styles and conventions, Skelton's parrot, no less virtuosic, parodies different ways of speaking. Imitating the multiplicity of parrot discourse, both works represent the sincerest form of flattery. But to return to Skelton: the power of Parott's political critique (of Cardinal Wolsey's influence on Henry VIII's foreign policy) depends on the multiplicity of his 'voice': besides speaking 'Frenshe of Paris, Dowche, Spanyshe, Englysshe', 'Yn Latyn, in Ebrue, and in Caldee,/ In Greke tong Parott can both speke and sey.' On top of which Parott also speaks a kind of lingua franca. As Parott boasts, 'Dame Phylology,/ Gave me a gyfte in my neste when I lay,/ To lerne all langage and hyt to speke aptly.'

More than this, Parott manipulates what he hears and relays, consciously introducing noise, as it were, into the poetic medium. The reason for this, Parott explains, 'Now *pandes mory* [perhaps meaning *prenez folie* or 'grow mad'], wax frantycke som men sey;/ Phronessys for frenyssys may not hold her way./ An almon now for Parott, delycatelye dreste;/ In *Salva festa dyes, toto* ys the beste.' Where ideology has corrupted and diminished the ordinary usages and resources of language, Parott's role is to restore these. Its Eve-like technique is, to assert the social value of those verbal 'paraphernalia' (gossip, hearsay, rumour, noise, diversity of dialects and the polyglots who parrot them) that defy all attempts at dumbing down and reduction to univocal sense. Parroting

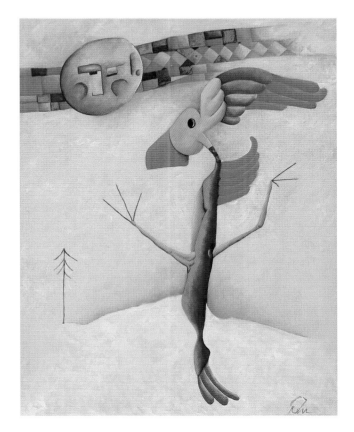

Attenuated or transfigured? David Derr's *Last Tango with Parrot* (2002), oil on canvas.

Society, Parott redefines rhetorical terms: 'of that supposicyon that calld is arte . . . Parrot nothing hath surmysed,/ No matter pretendyd, nor nothing enterprysed,/ But that *metaphora, alegoria* withall,/ Shall be his protectyon, his pavys and his wall.'

This seems to contradict what I said before – that parrots rely on contiguity, rather than metaphor, to suggest new ideas. But it seems that, in Parott's handling of them, metaphor and allegory are changed: 'in parabyll', Parott explains, addressing himself in the second person, 'ye wantonlye pronounce,/ Langagys divers; yet undyr that dothe reste/ Maters more precious than the ryche jacounce.'[125] In other words, as a *para*-speaker, skilled in the discourses of others, Parott doesn't need to invent far-fetched and artful connections. The talk of the many (of society) is intrinsically roundabout or parabolic. All that is needed to reveal its common sense (more valuable than the poet's artful and rare jewels of eloquence) is to repeat its diversity, showing that all the parts belong together, noise and all.

Para-talk, the discourse of those apparently parroting back what another has said, is the style of parodists, satirists, ironists, intelligent mimics, echoic doubles. As a compositional technique, in which a pattern or meaning is woven from a myriad of cast-off or traditional scraps, it is the technique of rhapsodists and ribald goliards improvising macaronic verse, of Euphuists and collage-prone Surrealists. The odd thing about the resultant babble is that, seeming to come from nowhere, it easily acquires other-worldly or spiritual qualities. Like the Mayan villagers, imagining Ya Lur's speech came from the world of the gods, so with the interpretation of para-talk generally: although generated externally, it comes to be identified with voices inside the head. Perhaps there is a psychological reason for this: the attenuated syntax that the Russian child psychologist Lev Vygotsky said characterized 'inner speech' exhibits the same terseness as the unadorned chatter of parrots. In any case, by a curious mutation, the noise of the everyday comes to intimate a transcendental meaning, communicated in silence. The raucous *parrhesia*, or plain-speech, of parrot the social critic becomes, mysteriously transfigured, the wordless voice of the *paraclete*, or Holy Spirit.

3 Parrotology

The argument of *Parrot* is not that the long history of parrot subjugation is a mirror in which we can see darkly inscribed our collective self-enslavement. No doubt this is true, but the recent history of almost any creature illustrates our imperialistic rapaciousness. Slaughter is the fate of any and all living things, including recalcitrant indigenous First Nations, standing in the path of the capitalistic juggernaut. The significance of parrots is not that they signify this or that failure of the collective imagination. It lies in showing how that collectivity of representations is constructed and sustained.

We are unused to regarding 'the many' as a concept. Yet, as is clear from chapter Two, 'Parroternalia', parrot is constitutionally many. Heirs to an ideological tradition that identifies the real with qualities of unity, univocity and autonomy, we are consequently disposed to treat parrot (daimonic, polyvocal and flock-dependent) as unreal. In doing this, we make the fatal but convenient mistake of filtering out as 'noise' the original, non-redundant information parrot has for us, which is that 'society', and these days 'the media', have a 'voice', and do not simply parrot back what we feed into them.

As a variation on the medium-is-the-message, this is hardly an original claim. Its significance lies in the fact that it demonstrates that our systems of communication originate outside

Untimely – the Black-fronted parakeet is extinct and, poignantly, the first depiction of it (Sydney Parkinson, 1768–71) is unfinished.

ourselves. The success of parrot in colonizing our global network of shared significations invites us to redefine the boundaries of society and the media. It suggests that our mechanisms of communication (from simple face-to-face speech, to the telephone and the Internet) are parrot-like, and that in sifting the information they furnish us solely for detachable messages, we miss the most important, and obvious, fact: that they model a sustainable ecology of social relations, and that this discourse is not even a collective human artefact, but finds its larger echo in the signifying sensory cosmos of the natural world.

To listen to what 'society' is telling us, that we cannot be ourselves (singly or collectively) without staying in touch with the always excessive signs of the other, is the first premiss of parrotology. And its practical value might be illustrated in relation to those classic topics – parrot trading and parrot conservation.

TRADE PARROT

Most accounts of parrot trading treat it as a subset of the cage-bird trade in general but, considering parrots as symbols of the way we communicate with one another, we can approach the topic differently. There is not simply a trade *in* parrots: trade exists because of the possibility of endowing things with parrot-like attributes that fit them to be exchanged. These attributes are whatever allows the thing to be classified, evaluated. They are what makes a dumb thing eloquent so that it acquires interest. A talking bird, especially one that comes dressed in paradisal plumage, embodies this 'value-adding'. Engaging us sensuously, it stimulates communication, it motivates us to trade – to give, to gain and to regulate these processes for profit. No doubt these statements can be made about many 'useless' products of the natural world, but the pre-eminent place parrots have always had in exchange rituals attests to their unique powers of attractions. Parrots please, and in the absence of military power or material wealth, they bridge the gap between conqueror and conquered, master and slave, suitor and mistress, disenfranchised farmer and black-market racketeer.

Parrots have been trade items from the beginning. For instance, the parrots imported from Africa or South America before the nineteenth century were not necessarily wild:

> Several writers from 1558 to 1625 described a parrot that was bred by Brazilian Indians, the progeny being traded to Europeans. Called Anapuru, possibly after a municipality of that name in Mato Grosso, it may have been *vinacea* [Vinaceous Amazon].[1]

This, or another parrot, was value-added at source: 'What an intimacy', Levi-Strauss wrote about long-standing French-Brazilian relations, 'can we read into the fact that in 1531 the frigate *La Pélérine* brought back to France "six hundred parrots that already know a few words of French".'[2] A different method of preparing parrots for market is described by Pernetty who, in his *Voyage aux isles Malouines*, reports the production of multi-coloured parrots by plucking individual feathers from the young bird and injecting a potion at the root.[3] Bougainville received one that was 'a gaudy mixture of jonquil and lemon yellow, carmine red, crimson, dark green and bright blue'.

But what might be called the sustainable trade in parrots has not been confined to the birds that changed hands wherever European navigators encountered the human inhabitants of parrot lands, or to such traditional practices as the breeding of parrots for the domestic feather trade (a practice widespread throughout pre- and post-Columbian Meso-America); it extends

to the role that the symbolic exchange of parrots has played in the evolution of intellectual commerce. Under 'Parrotics' I gave the scanty fossil evidence from which scientists have attempted to extrapolate the parrot's evolutionary history. It is no accident that the earliest parrot progenitor (*Archaeopsittacus verreauxii*) is named after the collector Jules Verreaux, founder of Maison Verreaux, whose business was dealing in rare and unusual natural history specimens and taxidermy. Collectors like the Verreaux brothers, John Gould (who described between 300 and 328 new species of Australian birds) or Auguste de Saint-Hilaire in Brazil

Alarmed by the camera flash, a pair of stuffed Black-capped lories attempts to take flight. From New Guinea, they are said to be 'prolific in aviary surroundings'. And in museums?

did not simply satisfy a taste for the exotic: to a large extent, they produced the curiosity that they then exploited for profit.

The stimulus to acquire came in the first instance from the sheer brilliance of hue and ingenuity of form (when resurrected by the taxidermist) of what had been shot in distant parts. In calibrating this dazzling tide of massacre, evolutionary theorists like Charles Darwin and Alfred Russel Wallace were, in effect, fixing intellectual exchange rates. Grouping specimens into families and genera, and suggesting genealogies, they added value to them. But the cases of stuffed specimens, the folios of meticulously delineated feathers, claws and beaks to which they gave interest did not *follow* their theories; they were the symbolic forms that made these new ways of thinking, relating and communicating desirable.

Usually, the threatened extinction of many species of parrot is attributed to one of two causes: poaching or destruction of breeding habitats. Poaching is really only a pejorative name for a practice as old as imperialism: the scientific collectors shooting their way through the rainforests of Europe's tropical colonies had no more right to take the parrots of those climes than today's Mataco Indians trapping Yellow-winged Amazons for the northern hemisphere bird market. Environmental vandalism is a more recent phenomenon but, in the accelerating destruction of the Amazon rainforest, is now the leading drain on parrot numbers and diversity. In his recent study of the extinction of the Carolina parakeet, Noel Snyder reminds us, though, that it is artificial to hold these two causes apart. The accepted explanation for the demise of *Conuropis carolinensis* has always been that it was persecuted (shot and caged) to its collective death. But this fashionably masochistic account overlooks 'the many and diverse relationships of the Carolina Parakeet with the lowly cocklebur', a weedplant spread by white farming practices. Snyder wonders whether it was not the loss, but the gain, of a food source that sealed the parrot's fate: first, the cocklebur drew the bird to human habitations, and second, the toxicity of the plant may have made the parakeets vulnerable to exotic disease. This is speculative, but Snyder's conclusion, that the causes of extinction were multifactorial (and perhaps counter-intuitive) is a timely reminder that conservation strategies must take account of 'complicated and obscure relationships among species and between species and their environments'.[4]

In other versions of John Audubon's *Carolina Parakeets* more birds appear, as if completing the composition depended on completing the slaughter. The last known pair, called 'Incas' and 'Lady Jane', died in 1918 in Cincinnati Zoo.

Usually, though, conservation strategies are born in the heat of battle and cannot afford to be so subtle. In the well-documented case of the South Australian subspecies of the Glossy black cockatoo, the availability of high-quality drooping sheoak for foraging and large hollow-bearing eucalypts for roosting and nesting have been identified as critical to the bird's survival.

But while land clearance may be a major factor in this species' decline, there are, as the recovery plan indicates, many imponderables: low breeding success, nest-hollow competition, inbreeding and nest-robbing for the pet trade. Ironically, poaching has gained in popularity precisely because the South Australian subspecies is receiving increasing public attention, showing once again that the desire to gain greater possession of the bird conceptually (through a more nuanced taxonomy) is inextricably linked to the desire to possess the bird physically, by caging and taming it.

In less sedate environments the complicated and obscure relationships that Snyder evokes involve not only natural but human ecologies and their interrelation: the OCP pipeline under construction between Ecuador and Colombia simultaneously opens up to rapacious exploitation the ancestral territories of isolated indigenous peoples and a fragile terrain supporting more than 500 species of bird. A conceptual extinction can also be predicted and lamented: the unique symbolic role played by parrots in these affected indigenous cultures. The shaman-mediated identifications with macaws that form a prominent part of the religious life of these communities embodies 'a set of ecological principles . . . [which] formulate a system of social and economic rules that have a highly adaptive value in the continuous endeavour to maintain a viable equilibrium between the resources of the environment and the demands of society'.[5]

Efforts to save threatened species of parrot are often stimulated by the activities of the poachers who threaten their survival. Aviculturalists play down the impact of poaching on parrot numbers, but recent studies by the universities of Maryland and California found that nearly a third of the 145 parrot species in the neotropics (Mexico, Central and South America) are threatened, making them among the most endangered groups

of birds worldwide. Parrots fetch an average of $800 in the USA and the number of parrot chicks taken from the wild is estimated at up to 800,000 per year. Parrots are particularly sensitive to poaching because they have low reproductive rates. Based on existing studies of 21 parrot species in 14 neotropical countries, the biologist Timothy Wright and his colleagues were able to make a direct correlation between species decline and poaching. The overall poaching rate was 30 per cent and for four species it exceeded 70 per cent, a rate that, given low reproductive rates, must produce a rapid decline.

These studies also demonstrate the importance of the Wild Bird Conservation Act which became law in the US in 1993. Wright and his colleagues compared poaching in ten species before and after the 1992 US Wild Bird Conservation Act, which bans imports of threatened parrots. They found that this legal protection cut poaching rates from nearly 50 per cent to 20 per cent. This not only contradicts the pet trade's arguments, that limiting legal trade intensifies illegal trade (and poaching): it underlines the importance of introducing similar legislation in Europe, currently the largest market for Meso- and South American parrots.

This general picture is the result of collating hundreds, if not thousands, of field reports. You can find representative samples of these at the websites of any of the conservation organizations involved in parrot protection. The Research Centre for African Parrot Conservation website is particularly informative, but the World Parrot Trust, Loro Parque Fundaçion, the Conservation in Aviculture Society and the RARE Center for Tropical Bird conservation all offer the concerned world citizen rich pickings. These organizations cross-reference one another, cooperate in jointly funding field projects, and mobilize an impressive diversity of talents, interests and expertises. Loro Parque (which also boasts the largest caged parrot population in the world) commits itself to supporting 'community-based conservation, education and sustainable development programmes that use parrots as flagships for the protection of the most endangered ecosystems', and it is quite savvy about the need to foster 'rainbow alliances' between groups whose interests formerly diverged. It aims, for example, 'to use captive-bred parrots in a sustainable manner to secure financial resources for conservation activities in the field, and to support re-introduction programmes'.[6]

As this last ambition illustrates, parrot conservation is strategic. The tactical focus of this strategy is the *species*: campaigns to win the hearts and minds of sceptical government ministers, resource market-dependent local communities, captains of industry and the Internet-literate public are fought at the species level, the banners of these media battles sporting images of individual birds. Whether it is the St Vincent parrot (in 1994 the World Parrot Trust sent one of its four 'Parrot Buses, created in partnership with Paul Butler of RARE Centre, to St Vincent, where it is used to educate the island's children about the importance of preserving the remaining rainforest'),[7] the Thick-billed parrot (a habitat-preservation initiative that involves paying the logging-dependent community 'a "rent payment" representing over time 50 per cent of the net value of the timber that will not be harvested')[8] or the Cape parrot (whose conservation strategy involves not only habitat conservation and 'effective policing of the bird trade' but also a captive bird breeding programme and 'provisioning of nesting boxes in the wild'),[9] or any of dozens of other parrot species, the unit of communication is one or two eye-catchingly beautiful birds, anthropomorphically endowed with personalities, biographies and a kind of *joie de vivre* that we can hardly resist.

Using advertising techniques to promote parrot conservation is often a simple, disarming means to a more complex environmental end. As Loro Parque says, because of their physical and psychological appeal, parrots can be 'flagships' symbolizing the need to protect entire ecosystems. Likewise, by turning 'the virtually anonymous St Vincent parrot into an island

Gorail, the name John Hunter gave to his picture of the Eastern rosella, was applied by the Aborigines of Sydney Cove to at least seven species of parrot, each of which had its own name (*Gorail* referred to a family).

superstar', a climate of opinion was created in which wildlife legislation was amended and CITES was ratified as well as a new captive parrot amnesty.[10] Yet the means they use is parrot trading by another name: signs may have been substituted for netted and drugged birds, but the object is the same – to create an interest in the parrots that is profitable in meeting the promoter's ends. The representation of parrots in this way is essential to their re-evaluation as symbols. It is as symbols that they can be exchanged, transported, sold on and value-added in other environments. But it is a moot point whether this acquisition of interest is in parrot's own long-term interest.

146

The hydroelectric project in the basin of the Tocantins River in Brazil floods an area of approximately 2,400 square kilometres. It is expected, though, that some 600 'islands' will be left when the new dam reaches its full extent. Developers argue: although the habitat of the Queen of Bavaria's conure will be destroyed, these islands will provide the species with a safe haven. Informed birdwatchers reply that this ignores the bird's behaviour.

> In the morning you would see a typical patch of virgin rainforest with disturbed but still active monkeys, birds, etc. By the afternoon there would be nothing but bare soil and very little sign of life. One would think that the fauna had moved on but the contractors tended to isolate a patch and come in with bulldozers from all sides. The birds appeared to be very reluctant to fly away even when the trees they were in were actually being felled.'

If this situation is tragic, isn't the conservation strategy proposed unduly comic? It is suggested that 'the birds from the area to be flooded [should] be trapped and sold abroad. Earnings . . . would be placed in a fund designated for proper maintenance and improvement of reserves.'[11] How, though, is the future of the Queen of Bavaria's conure served by an exchange that not only destroys its way of life but removes any last obstacle to deforestation?

This story reveals a weakness in conservation strategies that mimics those of the interests they oppose. When conservationists use the same language (and imagery) as multinational companies defending their profits and live bird collectors stocking their aviaries, they fall into a narcissistic discourse in which the fulfilment of individual desire is substituted for the subtler (but

The Crimson rosella was at first named after the English ornithologist Thomas Pennnant, as in Sarah Stone's *Pennantian Parrot*, 1790. The painting classifies the new Australian parrot as an 'uneven' or wedge-tailed type.

greater) erotic satisfaction of enriching the common good. The main reason for the extinction of the Spix's macaw, as has recently been shown with excoriating clarity, is the selfishness of private individuals.[12] To elide self-identification with the plight of a (non-human) other, a strategy no different from the one advertising agencies use to encourage identification with objects, is to perpetuate a traditional relationship with parrots, one based on the parent–child, master–slave or spectator–jester models. Omitted from this conception of parrot knowledge is what parrots can teach us. And *this* emerges as soon as parrots are considered not as trade items but as informants about the nature of exchange.

In the context of criticizing a rhetoric that risks devaluing what it intends to prize, it is interesting to consider the ambiguity of the term 'plume'. Used as a verb, *plume* can mean to decorate a body with feathers *or* to pluck the feathers from a body. It can also mean to dress oneself with borrowed plumes. A long, bloody and arithmetically astounding cultural history could be sheeted into this ambiguity. In Britain, Mearns and Mearns write:

> the plumage industry was an important part of the national economy and it has been estimated that from 1870 to 1920 twenty thousand tons of ornamental plumage entered the country each year. The most popular species were herons and egrets (for 'osprey' plumes), birds of paradise, cock o' the rocks, parrots, toucans, trogons and hummingbirds. In London, which was the centre of the trade, one dealer sold two million wild bird skins in just one year.

The New York market could have furnished similar figures, the whole trade representing a cumulative 'direct impact on wild birds (as distinct from destruction of habitat) . . . so catastrophic that it led to the birth of the modern conservation movement'.[13] In any case, reconciling the mass slaughter of birds with the noble pursuit of human adornment, the feather trade has been another avenue through which we have dressed up an environmental tragedy as a tribute to art: in pursuit of a more seductive appearance, willingly sacrificing the deeper community we share with animals.

Non-Western communities have targeted parrot plumes more single-mindedly – and, in general, more sustainably. Meso- and South American cultures, where a polymorphic symbolism at once cosmic, ecological, psychological and social attaches to parrots, like to dress up their shamans in macaw feathers. A recent article reporting on the efforts in Colombia to set up 'a code of ethics against shams' was illustrated by a shaman wearing a bonnet of parrot feathers and a necklace of jaguar teeth 'as talismans of healing power'.[14] There was nothing quaintly primitive about this: accreditation as a shaman is part of an ongoing fight to revoke a patent that allows a California-based company to exploit the medicinal properties of a vine called *ayahuasca* used in Amazon religious rituals.

Still, even this more modest feather harvest can, in combination with pressures on habitat, produce serious decline. In this regard Silva describes a successful initiative to recycle the sacred plumes. Hearing that a population of the extremely rare Lear's macaw in south-west Panama was under threat from feather hunters – between 60 and 80 feathers were being collected each year to decorate masks used in a ceremony in honour of Corpus Christi – Silva suggested using moulted plumes from his own captive birds. Explaining that 'Demand made a lucrative trade for a hunter, who earns only $3.00 per diem', Silva writes that now 'Feathers are rented to dancers, which would normally pay $3.50 each.'[15] How the hunters have supplemented their income is not stated.

If the conservation of parrots is to avoid the ambiguity of its own terms – the preservation of existing conditions easily morphing into an anti-social vision of collections reserved for the very few – then the role parrots play as symbols of communica-

George Shaw called this Crimson rosella 'The Splendid Parrot' in the early 1790s. This name has since migrated to another species, *Neophema splendida*, or Splendid parakeet, found in the arid interior of Australia.

tion needs to be understood. I would like parrots promoted as symbols of society. I would like their cybernetic genius recognized, for parrots are not only traded, they steer trade. Reflecting back to us our desire of exchange, they show us that communication always exceeds what is exchanged. Parrots show us that the globalized collective imaginary, and the communication systems that articulate it, are ecologically structured (and not simply an aggregate of privately addressed and received messages).

Here, constitutionally many, parrots are symbols. In the information transfer process, they function like synapses. The repetitions that are never quite the same are poetic techniques of community-building: meaningless in themselves, they create the environment in which communication is possible. These parrot associations are not secondary: they are cognate with the earliest exchanges between parrots and humans. If culture is communication, they define parrot culture as the collective awareness of communication as ecologically structured. Learning how we impoverish our grasp on the world when we inhabit our sign systems neglectfully is a critical preliminary to framing a conservation vision that is poetically, as well as strategically, coherent and sustainable.

ALEXIA

One scientist who has been listening (for nearly 40 years) to parrots (or at least to Alex, her African grey) is Dr Irene Pepperberg. Like her subject, Pepperberg is an outstanding communicator: a continuous stream of scientific papers, an active website and innumerable popular reports about her findings attest to an extraordinary single-mindedness of purpose. At the start of the project in June 1977 Alex was thirteen months old 'and had received no prior vocal instruction'. By the time he was 20 years old he had learned to name more than 35 objects; he knew the meaning of 'No', could use appropriately phrases of the type 'I want X' and 'Wanna go Y'; he could identify seven colours, five different shapes and quantities of objects. Most impressively, he could combine (with an accuracy of 80 per cent or higher) 'all the vocal labels to identify proficiently, request, refuse, categorize, and quantify more than 100 different objects, including those that vary somewhat from training exemplars'. Pepperberg has found that Alex's interspecific communicational abilities rival those of whales, seals and sea-lions. In her more recent work, she has studied a new phenomenon, the possibility that Alex is, in effect, responding critically to the experimental situation, in this sense mimicking what the scientists want to hear.

It seems indisputable that Pepperberg has made her point – parrots (Alex at least) are not 'mindless mimics', they are able to 'engage in complex, meaningful communication'. But what is the significance of this? To produce her results Pepperberg has used, adapted and ingeniously applied a variety of training techniques and testing procedures borrowed from human learning studies and from earlier studies in parrot ethology. Education is object-based, Alex learning the names of objects by observing his human trainers handling and talking about them. Rewards are used to induce Alex to take part in the experiments, and these are quite subtle: if Alex successfully identifies 'cork', he may request (correctly) a different reward ('I want banana'). The aim at every point is to isolate Alex from anything likely to distract him from the present experimental task. It is as if his environment has to be blanked out in order for him to concentrate.

The experiments in object-name association also depend on eliminating any empathetic collusion between bird and human. To ensure that Alex is responding to the question (and not to 'inadvertent cuing') the trainers mix up questions, even make mistakes and indulge in various games ('an important protocol because Alex becomes restless during sessions devoted to single tasks'). Creativity is not ruled out but is regarded as a sign of intelligence only when it leads to an extended grasp of objects: 'novel vocalizations' produced 'spontaneously' (after Alex learned 'grey', he also said 'grape', 'grate', 'grain', 'chain', and 'cane') are regarded as meaningless. Rather than evaluate 'their intentionality', 'trainers respond to the novel speech acts as though he were intentionally commenting about or requesting objects, actions, or information'.

Against this background of obstacles to communication, it seems (from the outside) that Alex's intelligence resides chiefly in his ability to intuit the rules of the game. Pepperberg says that the initial premises of her study were that parrots communicated in the wild ('vocalizations appear to mediate social interactions between mated pairs and among flock members') and that 'natural behaviours would not differ greatly from what had been observed in captivity'.[16] Without questioning either premiss, it's clear that Pepperberg's laboratory resembles neither the wild nor an ordinary aviary (where interspecific communication, if any, is infantile). Exemplifying Kant's criticism of empirical science in general, Pepperberg's experimental situation proves mainly that her experiments work.

They work because of a strange untested assumption, which is that Alex will mimic his trainers *knowingly*, that he will internalize what they do, and identify it with his own desire, in this way learning to behave in a non-mimetic, self-motivated way. But so long as mimicry is, on the one hand, used to teach, and on the other hand, discouraged in the student (the disregard of Alex's phonic sound-alikes), learning can only ever be mimicry. If the parrot's own flock-oriented communicational ambitions are deliberately misunderstood, its intelligence (its gift for survival) depends on developing a certain stoical resignation, and an ironic awareness that an inverse relation exists between his success in performing them and his capacity to communicate intelligently (about the system). That is, the more he imitates their desires, the less his desire of communication can be communicated. Since this desire is profoundly mimetic, originating in a doubling with interest of the other's voice, its systematic punishment represents a cruel dumbing-down. It is odd to think that the same ironies inform the public education of children throughout the Western world.

indexed, or Blue bellied Parrot. Latham Syn..... 1 p 212

Showing off: Thomas Watling's mid-1790s rendering of a Blue-bellied or Red-breasted parrot (our Rainbow lorikeet) is yet another variation on bringing a still life to life.

When Pepperberg wanted to test whether parrots could recognize themselves in mirrors, she had to exclude Alex because 'long before this project was initiated, he had essentially been taught that the image he saw in the mirror was "Alex"'.[17] This is an experimental irony that suggests that those apparently different concepts – 'recognition', 'self', object-name relations – are tautologous. Leaving that aside, there is a more generic difficulty associated with having parrots look at themselves in mirrors. The classic test for self-recognition is difficult to conduct on parrots. It involves putting a coloured mark on a part of the subject's body that it cannot see without the use of a mirror. If the subject looks at its reflection and touches the mark on its body, instead of the mirror image, it has demonstrated that it knows the image in the mirror is a reflection of itself. The physical

arrangement of the parrot's eyes, though, makes this test next to impossible. With one eye it can see one side of itself; with the other eye it can survey the other side. But, unlike us, parrots have no unified image of themselves formed by stereoscopic synthesis. There is, physiologically, no reason why parrot should 'think' of itself as possessing a single identity, and hence no reason why any part of it should be out of sight.

Parrot resists the mirror test because its bilaterality is a condition of its self-perception. It cannot be mirrored in a mirror because its two sides do not mirror each other but are different – the parrot's two fields of vision, for example, can never be focused into a single image. Parrots, like other birds, can form a coherent 360-degree image of their environment, but, unlike ours, it is not predicated on crushing laterality into a perspectival cage. It involves an effortless assimilation of continuously heterogeneous prospects into a view without centre or edge. Curiosity about the supposed bilaterality of parrots is one of the oldest topics in the modern parrot literature, but its motivation has been characteristically anthropomorphic. The belief that parrots are left-footed, preferentially perching on the right foot and holding the foot with the left, can be found in Sir Thomas Browne. Writing against the 'vulgar error' that right-handedness was natural, he asserted a 'prevalency ofttimes in the other' (i.e., the left side) in certain animals whose 'forelegs . . . supply the want of armes'. The animals in question included squirrels, monkeys and 'Parrets'.[18] FCH, a contributor to *Notes and Queries* in 1869, had 'heard it affirmed that the male parrot always holds anything to eat in his right foot, and that the female as regularly uses the left'.[19]

Debate about parrot laterality was stimulated in 1865 when Paul Broca proposed that cerebral control for speech as well as for manual dexterity (right-handedness) lay in the left cerebral hemisphere.[20] Broca was also prepared to entertain the idea that animals might also show 'dysmmetry of the convolutions'. When the British neurologist William Ogle watched 86 parrots in the London zoological gardens, he found that 63 supported themselves on the right leg while eating a nut out of the left.[21] The American zoologist David Starr Jordan, conducting his own experiments, concluded that left-footedness 'is due entirely to the

In his Eastern rosella of 1794, James Sowerby combines poses used by his fellow Sydney artists.

fact that those who offer the finger or food to parrots do so as a rule with the right hand'. Besides, 'does perching on right, holding with left, mean that the parrot is left-footed or right-footed?'.[22]

Why should so arcane a topic have attracted so much interest: 'Although current neuropsychological opinion about parrot footedness rests on just two reports [dating from 1938 and 1980], the literature on this subject is remarkably extensive.'[23] The interest is only partly 'scientific': informing it is a fantasy about the humanness of parrots, an idea that they share our capacity for lateral thinking. The main argument for this is that the cerebral specialization for footedness is also implicated in vocal production. To attribute bilaterality to parrots is to qualify them to speak. A survey of parrot owners in 1949 found that left-footed parrots (mainly African greys or Amazons) were significantly more frequent among those that spoke more than 70 words[24] – did this prove footedness or document the lexicon of the parrot owners? But there is no end to this speculation. Crimson, Eastern and pale-headed rosellas are apparently right-footed: are they avian pierrots, parodying their left-footed brethren, chattering back to front? Poor *Aratiga pertinax* exhibits no footedness at all: unable to put its best leg forward, it is forever stuttering.[25]

Right- or left-footed: George Edwards's Red and blue-headed parakeet, 1751.

These empirically based readings of parrot behaviour seem to me curiously lobotomized. Left out is the investigator's self-interest, and – what follows from this – the desire that the subject bird mimic the investigator's expectations. Also left out is the environment, which, in ordinary circumstances, is the reason for communication. The lexicon that a laboratory parrot learns, the tricks that a caged bird masters, are the elements of a miniature drama that faithfully reflects the prison of their production. To receive these data and to interpret them at face value is to exhibit what might be called a kind of *alexia*. This is not to disparage the findings of animal behaviourists and comparative psychologists, but simply to reiterate that 'parrot knowledge' may be something very different from knowing about parrots.

Watching the parrot swaying side to side in his cage, I would risk hypothesizing a very different kind of bilateral intelligence at work. Buffon said the parrot was particularly wary of hunters – seeing a companion fall to the gun, it cries out at the top of its voice.[26] Seeing us look at it in its cage, it seems similarly outraged. It may not cry out, but it communicates its unease by bobbing to left and right. Insisting on the asymmetrical leftness and rightness of his existence, he is still weighing up where he belongs.

Just as the parrot's glance is sidelong, so with the eye science turns on the parrot: it focuses on the bird's maximum spread, its lateral exposure. Science's parrot is always flying by or fixing you with a single eye. In the interests of capturing such identifying features as distinctively coloured cheeks, shoulders, wings and tails, imperialism's parrots lack frontality: an arrowhead offers no target – the shooter holds fire until his quarry swerves away from encounter, exposing a brilliant flank. The longitudinal symmetry of the parrot's plumage eludes this point of view. A trivial oversight? Not from the parrot's point of view. It misses the environmental efficiency of his colouring. It also disparages the pragmatic virtues of the vertical assymmetry of the parrot's patterning, the contrast between back and belly, upper- and under-wing. The scientific point of view makes a clown of the parrot, as if his rainbow design were both a caprice and a folly. Small wonder so foolishly attired a spirit should attract attention. His self-advertisement invites capture, enslavement and display.

Naturally, there is evolution: while John Audubon used to shoot a bird and pin it up on a board for sketching, John Gould showed not only the birds in natural positions, but plants, trees and foliage. But, of course, the naturalness is both posed and composed. The addition of a mate and a branch or two suggestive of the jungle only increases the vicarious sense of exposure. The duller female of the species characteristically perches the opposite way behind her mate. The crossed figure suggests a hierarchically devised Christian marriage. These are 'lovebirds' who have tied the knot of lifelong devotion. The perspectival illusion enlarges the male relative to the smaller female. He assumes the human role of chivalrous protector. Anthropomorphism also emerges in the

erect posture in which parrots are mounted and depicted. It ignores their characteristically creeping motion on ground or branch, and their pigeon-toed gait. Exposing their stubby legs and zygodactylic feet, ill-adapted to perching, it reduces the parrots to unathletic mannequins, stiff toy tin soldiers and finger puppets.

The identification of parrot knowledge with an art of exposure leads to curious paradoxes. What, for example, does it mean when, in his book *Extinct Birds*, Errol Fuller includes his own paintings of extinct parrots?[27] Plate 8 in Walter Rothschild's *Extinct and Vanishing Birds of the World* is a representation of *Necropsittacus borbonicus*, '⅖ths natural size', based on one sentence: 'This parrot is described by the Sieur D.B. (Dubois) in the following terms:- "Body the size of a large pigeon, green; head, tail and upper part of wings the colour of fire." The writer is candid enough to admit that 'This description is the sole evidence we have of the existence of this bird.' But this does not dull his desire to represent it: 'As he compares it with other parrots which are true Palaeornis, it is evident that this bird must have been a Necropsittacus.'[28] Other parrots

Lophopsittacus mauritianus or Blue parrot, 'last mentioned in 1680, first described in 1866' (*sic*), was first illustrated in Lord Lionel Walter Rothschild's *Extinct and Vanishing Birds of the World* (1909).

Counterfeit or composed? The convicted forger and artist Thomas Watling's incomparable ('Non-Pareil') parrot draws on poses, settings and a colour palette established by his Sydney contemporaries.

manage to flash across the eager eye of science only to retreat before they can be fixed. The New Caledonian diademed lorikeet, for instance, 'is known only from two females, one of which has apparently been lost'.[29] This does not inhibit painting a picture of the bird – a consoling image which, in its way, is more authoritative than any known sighting.

Paintings of extinct parrots are not only poignant. The imagination involved in their representation stirs up troubling thoughts. Is it the paradise of their hues that makes their extinction possible? In the underworld of extinction, another jungle thrives, other clearings thrilled by colourful birds in headlong flight. It is crowded there, and our destruction, posting new immigrants there, adds to its deathly vitality. In extinction's world, every parrot has its perch, where it eyes the hunter without fear. There is not a tree that doesn't sport the unique representative of its kind. They cannot breed there. But they are immortal, attaining what they could never achieve in cages, instalment in eternity.

In the realm of representation, there is no difference between images of dead parrots and living ones. The object of the art of exposure remains the same: to present a visual type specimen that will stand the test of time. Logically, the best-known (most definitively represented) parrots are the least known. Over time images of living parrots change. Further specimens or captive birds become available. The early, sometimes crude representations are superseded. Sometimes an original portrait is not surpassed, but the proliferation of later versions obscures its power, and the iconic force of the bird in the collective mind grows blurred and variable. Extinct parrots undergo no iconographic development or stylistic variation. The type specimen and the portrait of the soon-to-be-extinct bird are unique. The first painting to preserve its paradise of colour is the last. Because they die out too quickly to be reproduced again, they never experience the conundrum of becoming many. Their beauty never grows relative. In extinction, the parrot, and the idea of the parrot, are fused forever. This is why extinct parrots are most beautiful: they are one with their Platonic form.

In this sense, the portraits of parrots, extinct or living, commemorate the paradox of discovery. Extinction is not discovery's accidental, tragic endgame. It resolves the crisis of discovery itself, where finding is dialectically twinned with loss. Discovery laboriously hauls hidden things to the light. But what is to hold them there, blinking in the clearing of reason? Too

unreliable to release, they must be killed, skinned and painted if they are to stay. The parrot's portrait represents the crisis of discovery. *Reproduction* signifies crisis – if there were no fear of loss there would be no rush to fix them with images. A recent newspaper report about threatened species was curiously entitled 'Extinct crisis'.[30] Presumably 'Extinction' was meant. But perhaps not: when a species of parrot dies out, it is, from science's point of view, a *crisis* that has become extinct. For the dread of loss, which has haunted it ever since the bird was discovered, is at last extinguished.

These premonitions of disappearance are detectable in the iconographic conventions of parrot representation. Painted poses and perches seem to foresee death. The parrot turning back to look at the painter gives the impression that the bird is

In the wake of efforts to represent Australian parrots typically, Richard Browne's swaying, snake-necked King parrots (1813) are *naif*, but they are also a rearguard attempt to represent the movement of things *outside* the cage of representation.

about to take flight. The shooter must see every bird like this, surprised, crouched, watchful, about to spring from its perch and take wing. He levels his gun before it can decide, and brings it down. Painted in this pose, the parrot is the figure of the hunter's desire. There is a genre of illustration that represents the parrot gripping a gnarled branch in the crown of a similarly gnarled tree. Old-fashioned, anomalous, eccentric, he is of no more use to the progress of society than a ruined abbey or Romantic traveller. But for the preserving charity of the Picturesque artist's taste, he would have become extinct long ago. The storm clouds gathering overhead presage as much.

As the menagerie of parrots lost to science increases, the ingenious parrot breeder counterpoises their extinction with a growing repertoire of utopian types. The caprices of his curious art may be truer to nature's originals than nature's evolving forms – it has been said that, in comparison with the offspring of Golden-shouldered and Mulga parrot matings, the now extinct Paradise parrot was 'no more than a naturally occurring hybrid'.[31] But, whether his cinnamon and hyacinth novelties are ancient or modern, they suggest Paradise regained. In this sense the aviary is Paradise itself – with this oddity, that here God's only law is change, his only criterion of selection what is beautiful in his, the godlike beholder's eye. His parrots are a chequerboard of potential chromatic combinations. He does the work the old creator didn't have time to do, working out all the possible combinations. In this sense he labours behind the scenes of creation. He is divinity's quality controller, critically recreating lost opportunities.

Scientists suspect these overnight creations of mocking their own hard-won productions. Their variability blunts science's thrust: where reproduction brings uncertain results, who can say if one is, or is not, another? Without origin elsewhere, with-

166

out *originals* elsewhere, these after-images of nature defy description. Holding no cryptic clue to 'nature', they avoid the crisis of discovery. They slip through representation's net. This is their triumph, to turn 'the flight from reality' into a cloak of invisibility – under hyaline hues to conceal their true colours. But the professional zoologist's unease may have another cause: these olive, jade, laurel and cinnamon mutations – some with plum-coloured eyes – strewn in the path of parrot knowledge, not only get in the way: they make manifest the repressed desire of science, not to understand parrots in their diverse places but to restore them to an ideal location in the human imaginary.

Are the extinctions of parrots marked? What happened to the parrot destined to become the type specimen of its race at length overtakes the species as a whole. History has made smoking chimneys and mushroom clouds icons of mass murder. The extinctions of parrots also deserve their meteorological portents. After hours spent amid the gloom of museum cabinets, studying greed's historical road-kill, I have gone outside and, looking up at the bright clouds, thought I saw the parrots' doom enacted there. Late afternoon cirrus, ahead of a storm front, morphs into cockatoo feathers, consolidates into a plumaged mass – until, like a slow albino firework, or a giant hand letting go, the shining body inexorably and irretrievably explodes. The track the wounded parrot-soul takes is visible later in the west. Giant feather-down hangs in the sky, galah-pink, coral and dusky mauve, but the dominant impression is of drops of blood.

I have imagined an exhibition of parrots devoted to the evolution of the idea of exposure. It would take its cue from one of Sidney Nolan's diary musings:

In the East one painter has devoted his life to the painting of a single type of bird. We could do the same here. Where for instance are the paintings of the long-lost Night-Parrot, so rarely seen now that an example is worth a hundred pounds. In passing one can paint them in such a

Hope abandoned: Sidney Nolan captures the irony of the name, *Pretty Polly Mine*, in his 1948 painting (acrylic on board) by identifying it with the Yellow-tailed black cockatoo, whose scientific name (*Calyptorhynchus funereus*) is anything but jolly.

story as Burke and Wills, but that is a different matter from the devotion one bird merits from a painter.[32]

The invisibility of night parrots has intrigued poets like Lavinia Greenlaw and Dorothy Porter. Indeed, Porter, who casts the night parrot as the daimon of her desire, is drawn to it precisely because it is not like the parrots 'At dusk / all over the world . . . screaming/ and squabbling/ in high trees' – 'shortly/ they'll shut up/ and settle for the night/ not like the night parrot/ who, on occasion, has stood at my window/ like an elegant Count Vampire'.[33] But mine would be a haunting vision of a different kind.

It would be about a different parrot vision, a night vision that respected the general invisibility of parrots. Suppose that parrot plumage fulfils either or both Darwinian functions, of sexual attractiveness and camouflage? Then parrot's visual culture (as opposed to ours) is tactical and situational. In general, parrots are retiring or flock at such great distances from the

human observer that their colours cannot be made out in any detail. Outside the pages of books and the stultifying lens of the camera, they are usually seen glancingly, captured peripherally, or embedded in the *chiaroscuro* labyrinth of foliage. They are rarely grasped as separate creatures, detachable from their backgrounds. They shine out like stars in the dark.

No parrots might appear in this exhibition at all, but they would be implied everywhere. They would be concealed in an installation documenting the debris of imperial retreat. Here, as 'stuffed parrots under bell-glasses', they would be classified with 'jars porcelain, china, and delft; shells, spars . . . glasses; corals, minerals and an infinity of trumpery'.[34] They would be the universal eye looking back whose primary colours squawk for attention in the works of artists otherwise as diverse as Miró, Mondrian and Jackson Pollock. Their flocks would be noticed drifting

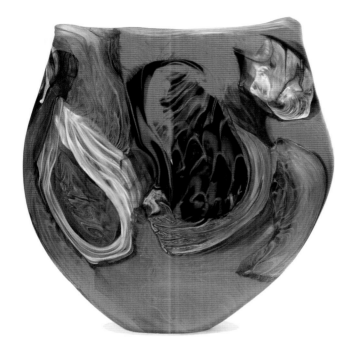

In a Glass
Alchemically:
Noel Hart,
Scarlet Rosella
vase, 2004.

through Renaissance charts and Pre-Raphaelite paintings as the polychromatic principle that holds the imagery together.

If such an exhibition could make us see seeing the way the parrot does, the first thing we might notice is not the parrot but the cage through which we look at it.

COLLECTING HABITS

Earlier, I posed a question: why do we love parrots to death? How can the destruction of their natural habitats, their physical, psychological and emotional enslavement and their genetic manipulation coexist in the collective imaginary with images of them as human like us – witty, sardonic, seeking companionship, given to laughter as well as self-pity? Why is our care so careless, our love so loveless? The answer may reside in our collecting habits. To say 'parrot' is already, it seems, to imagine collecting it. Naming is associated with the idea of classification, discipline and displacement. Representation implies the destruction of what resists representation. It is a strange love that drives us to infantilize our captives, to breed out their personalities and substitute our own. Perhaps it should be called guilt. The scientists' zoos, the aviculturalists' aviaries, the companion-bird person's cage: they are ersatz states of being. The collecting habit they embody represents unsatisfied love.

Representations fail to meet our emotional needs. Highlighting the unattainability of the other, they fuel anger and violence, which can be tamed only when the other is tamed (or destroyed). John James Audubon described the slaughter of Carolina parrots or parakeets:

> The gun is kept at work; eight, or ten, or even twenty, are killed at every discharge . . . I have seen several hundreds destroyed in this manner in the course of a few hours, and have procured a basketful of these birds at a few shots, in order to make choice of good specimens for drawing the figures.[35]

Back in the studio, he had to work fast to counter their deterioration. In our own day, Joseph Forshaw, author of the monumental *Parrots of the World*, displays the same mindset. His interest in birds began as a schoolboy, when he spent his weekends 'trapping Zebra finches *Taeniopygia guttata* and Red-rumped Parrots *Psephotus haematonotus* in market gardens on the river-

banks'. Early experiences like these, he comments, 'explain the deep-rooted affinity between Australian aviculturalists and native species'.[36] How can the distress caused to birds through trapping and caging them be a sign of 'affinity'? The answer seems plain: collecting birds affords an experience of kinship, an ersatz intimacy, unattainable when the birds fly free.

A feature of these collecting habits is a blocked desire of communication. It is the sullen dumbness of nature that provokes a lust to possess it. Here the distinction of parrots emerges. Parrots do communicate. But instead of letting them teach us how to communicate differently, we cage them inside our own, strictly utilitarian economy of signs. We imagine them like ourselves, as self-sufficient states, instead of entertaining the possibility (embraced, for example, in Meso-American

Ara-chronistic: macaws (arara) can be removed in space (p. 143) or time, as in Frans Frencken the Younger, *The Young Ulysses' Recognition of Achilles among the Daughters of Lycomede*, early 1700s.

culture) that parrot talk is constitutionally excessive, its social utility residing in the fact that (in terms of information-transfer) it is useless, its chatter purely ornamental or erotic. In this spirit, the poet Peter Steele promotes the re-evaluation of parrot as 'pure ornament'. Being priceless, the usual collars, manacles and cages of exchange would not apply to them. Freed from 'the tortoiseshell and silver,/ the ivory of caging Rome', they might be free to assume a new cultural role, representing collectively 'a making free with each piratical shoulder,/ as popinjay or Papageno'.[37]

We might come back to plumes, whose signification in seventeenth-century European representation Joseph Roach interprets in terms of Georges Bataille's notion that human cultures are structured around the management of superabundance. Referring to their theatrical popularity (Addison complained that 'The ordinary method of making a Heroe is to clap a huge Plume of feathers upon his head'),[38] Roach argues:

> in the 'General Economy' of the heroic play the performance of waste, enacted amid the haunted vestiges of the European spirit world, occurred on the level of material extravagance in adornment, especially feathered plumes, as well as blood. As a material object, the feather masks an act of violence: what it cost to produce was the original wearer's life, and what it served to dramatize was the predication of overarching symbolic systems on the material basis of waste.[39]

Feathers represented conspicuous consumption or luxury because of the sacrifice they implied. They stood for hedonistic or irresponsible excess. They celebrated the prospect of extinction, justifying the destructive character of life.

Pollyphonic, or the best of talking machines: *Le Gramophone* by Louis Charles Bombled, Paris, c. 1930.

The collecting habits of *Parrot* have mimicked their subject. Stories about parrots, allusions to them in myth, in the scientific literature and in nursery tales have been collected for no better reason than the sound and sight of the name. The poet Thomas Nashe and the Elizabethans fancied that almonds were needed to motivate parrots: my 'almonds' have been 'parrots', the word, where it occurred in subject indexes, Internet searches, online picture libraries.

That I *could* proceed in this way reflected the nature of contemporary information organization and retrieval. Gone are the days when data was organized locally, thematically and genealogically. In the pre-electronic library only an exceptionally zealous parrotologist would have located both a Jataka story about parrots and an article (published in a professional journal of psychology) on right- and left-footedness in parrots. But now a cosmos of inscrutable hearsay, anecdote, opinion – with nothing else in common than its susceptibility to recovery via the talismanic name 'parrot' – can be gathered: Mozart's Papageno as the first modern account of Down syndrome, the prehensile feats of the Trained Parrot Circus, the fate of the nestling yellow-winged Amazons traded in the Argentinian province of Chaco, and a painting by George Morland (*The Disconsolate and her Parrot*).

Isn't this an eloquence that collapses into noise, an omniscience so superficial that it universalizes ignorance? Isn't this also the challenge of the parrot, that it defies classification, shadow-boxing our searches, tempting our fantasies and ultimately defeating our definitions? Is this the apocalypse of meaning of which the parrot has been warning ever since we caged it and, captivated by its mimicry, taught it to talk? Remember Dusky, who bides his time before beginning very slowly 'Hee . . . hee . . . hee', causing his owners to 'crack up' and the whole thing to start again?[40] Isn't this how the whole thing will end? When humanity finally gets the joke? Isn't this what the parrot is waiting for?

And yet a universe of associations that is coherent emerges. As the alphabestiary suggested: if each parrot association generates a multiplicity of further associations (so that it's impossible to nominate an original fact), yet each radiating strand forms a knot with a group of others. In this network of parroternalia everything does seem to join up, and the pattern woven through the information does seem to constitute a kind of knowledge. The fact that, when viewed in the global perspective of contemporary information retrieval, parrot attributes transcend dialectical classification is significant. It is as a mirror to the polymorphic character of desire – suppliant, cruel, self-sacrificing, destructive, narcissistic – that parrot matters. The object of this book is not to subtract pleasure from our contract with parrot. It is to consider the fact that parrot parents, describes and classifies our worldly pleasures.

Neither outside us (for there is no place where parrot can live apart from our interference), nor inside us (for there is a polysemous indifference to identity that renders the parrot 'public' even in private), parrot could mediate a new deeply human covenant with the global environment. But he won't preside over this new world until we own our parrot nature. A profound unseriousness, a tragic playfulness, a democratizing irony, the admission to the negotiating table of an imagination that we take for reality: these will be the qualities of the players who can avoid the endgame. Parrots will then play the role we always wanted them to play. Standing at their shoulder, overlooking their deliberations, as they discuss the reparation of historical wrongs and environmental expropriations, myriad cultural genocides and biological tamperings, what will we do? Persist in the myth that they repeat what we say?

Or will we admit the obvious, that in the benevolence of their squawking laughter they offer us a different way of understanding reality, one in which noise does not drown out tenderness, attachment and regret but, rather, amplifies it in so many directions that it becomes a new jungle, one where communication and culture are not linked by an = sign but whose relationship resembles the net? Irony keeps the web tense, and the serious play involved in maintaining peaceable relations. We have a lot to learn. Parrot can teach us.

Ferdinand Bauer, Northern or Brown's Rosella, Shot at Caledon Bay, Arnhem Land, Northern Territory, 6 February 1803.

Timeline of the Parrot

C. 65–70 MILLION YEARS BC

Oldest known parrot and oldest reported modern land bird, described from lower jaw, 'probably from a bird about the size of a macaw'

C. 50 MILLION YEARS BC

Psittacopes lepidus, described from a skeleton found in Germany; of similar date is *Pulchrapollia gracilis gen*, described from a tarsometatarsus found in London Clay in England

C. 30 MILLION YEARS BC

Archaeopsittacus verreauxii, described from tarsometatarsus found near Allier, France

1000 BC

Parrots mentioned in the Rig Veda

397 BC

The earliest known reference to a parrot in European literature is in Ctesias' *Indica*, a fairly accurate description of a Plum-headed parakeet

C. 350 BC

In his *History of Animals*, Aristotle (385–322 BC) describes a similar bird (parakeet?) which he called *Psittace*

50 BC

Diodorus Siculus, a Roman, writes of the parrots he has seen in Syria

1402

The French report African greys in the Canaries (they had been imported from West Africa)

1493

Columbus, following his epic voyage to the New World, brings back a pair of Cuban Amazons for his patron, Queen Isabella of Spain

1521

John Skelton's 'Speke Parott'

1821

Heinrich Kuhl publishes his *Conspectus Psittacorum* of 209 species of parrot (18 of them new to science)

1830

Edward Lear publishes the first part of *Illustrations of the Family of Psittacidae, or Parrots*

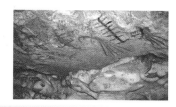

C. 20 MILLION YEARS BC

Conuropsis fratercula, described from a left humerus found in Nebraska

C. 20 MILLION YEARS BC

Presumed diversification of genera during the Miocene, and of species within genera during the Pliocene and Pleistocene

3000 BC

Cave paintings of macaws, Soledade Rock, Rio Grande do Norte State, north-east Brazil

2ND–9TH CENTURIES

Nazca geoglyph of parrot

7TH–9TH CENTURIES

Macaw petroglyphs, Anazazi National Monument, New Mexico.

C. 800–900

Earliest known sculptures of cockatoos, Prambanan Temple complex, Java

C. 1220

Frederick II of Hohenstaufen receives an Umbrella cockatoo from the Sultan of Babylon

1864

The last recorded Cuban macaw, one of the seven species of West Indian macaws, is shot from its perch

1980–92

247 species of parrot are reported in international trade, with 156 of them traded over that period in volumes exceeding 1,000 birds annually

1998

Juniper and Parr estimate that 90 species of parrot are under threat, 81 per cent from habitat loss, 43 per cent from trade, with at least 31 per cent threatened by both pressures

2050

Within 50 years only 5% per cent of parrot habitat will remain in 'Protected Areas'

Parrot Jokes

COURTEOUS PARROT

A lady was walking down the street to work and saw a parrot in a pet shop. She stopped to admire the bird. The parrot responded: 'Hey, you are *so* ugly!' The woman marched off in a huff. On the way home that evening she saw the same parrot, and the bird, on spotting her, again squawked 'Hey, you are *so* ugly!' She was incredibly annoyed now. The next day on the way to work the same thing happened. She stormed into the shop threatening to take the owner to court and have the parrot destroyed. The manager apologized profusely and promised the bird wouldn't say it again. So that evening, when she walked past the shop after work the parrot simply called out to her, 'Hey!' She paused, scowled, and with an icy stare said in a hoarse voice, 'Yes?' The bird slowly rocked back and forth on its perch. But eventually replied: 'Oh, *you* know . . .'.

GRINDER AND THE PARROT

Mrs Brown's dishwasher was broken, so she phoned an electrician. She told him: 'I'll leave the key under the mat. When you've fixed it, leave a bill in the kitchen and I'll mail you a cheque. By the way, don't worry about Rex, my rottweiler. He's very obedient. Does whatever we tell him. But, whatever you do, don't annoy the parrot. It's got a terrible temper.'

When the electrician arrived at Mrs Brown's house the next day, he discovered the biggest and scariest looking dog he'd ever seen. But, just as she had said, the rottweiler simply lay on the floor, watching the electrician getting on with fixing the dishwasher. However, the caged parrot never stopped screeching and squawking for a moment, and slowly drove the man nuts with all its noise.

Finally, he couldn't stand it any longer: 'Shut up, you horrible, stupid, ugly, brainless bird!' The parrot went insane with anger: 'OK,' it screamed, 'you've really done it now. *Get him Grinder!*'

CHILLING OUT

A young man named Jeff received a parrot as a gift. Unfortunately, this was a parrot with a bad attitude that used terrible language. Everything it said was crude and vile. Jeff tried and tried to make the bird behave, by constantly making polite conversation, playing soft music, in fact doing everything he could think of to set a good example. Nothing worked.

Eventually, one day Jeff lost his temper and yelled at the parrot. The bird simply yelled back. Jeff shook the parrot, but the bird just got angrier and ruder. Finally, desperate for a moment's silence, Jeff tore open the refridgerator door, stuffed the parrot inside, and slammed the door shut. For a minute or two, screaming, banging and dreadful cursing could faintly be heard coming from within the refridgerator, but the noise suddenly stopped. Completely.

Scared that he'd suffocated the bird, Jeff quickly opened the door. The parrot stumbled out and hopped onto the table: 'Jeff, I believe I may have offended you with my bad language and oafish behaviour. I am truly sorry, and will never, ever behave or speak badly again. *Ever*!'

Jeff was astonished at this inexplicable change of attitude. But while he was puzzling over what possibly could have brought it about, the contrite parrot broke in on his thoughts: 'Um, Jeff . . . , just out of interest . . . , uh, *what* exactly had the chicken done?'

A happy magician travelled the world on cruise ships as a highly popular entertainer. But, finally, on one cruise his luck ran out. The captain had insisted that his pet parrot be allowed to watch the musician's shows whenever it liked, and as a result the parrot learned all the routines off by heart. Now bored, the parrot began ruining the evenings for everyone by constantly calling out 'Uh, oh, watch his right hand, he's hidden it there!' or 'Any second he'll pull out yards of red bunting from that hat!', and so on. The magician was furious, and became depressed. But he didn't dare complain to the captain.

While crossing the Pacific, a huge storm blew up. It utterly overwhelmed the ship, which went down. No one survived, except the magician, who had managed to scramble into a lifeboat. And then the parrot fluttered into view and landed on his boat.

For three days and nights the magician and the parrot just glared at each other from opposite ends of the boat. Neither said a word. But finally, with a long drawn-out sigh the parrot spoke: 'OK, I give up. Where's the ship?'

References

INTRODUCTION: COMMUNICATING PARROTS

1 Hillel Schwartz, *The Culture of the Copy: Striking Likenesses, Unreasonable Facsimiles* (New York, 1996), p. 149.
2 Wallace Stevens, 'The Bird with the Coppery Claws', *Collected Poems* (London, 1966), p. 82.
3 The progressive elevation of parrots in nineteenth-century natural history elevation begins with John Gould; the imperial fantasy it represents is a story by itself.
4 In 1886 the ornithologist Frank Chapman surveyed 700 hats worn by New York ladies, finding that they contained feathers from no less than 160 North American species. As for the association of plumes with virility, in 1957 Sir David Attenborough estimated more than over 10,000 birds had been killed to furnish headdresses for 500 dancers attending ceremonies he witnessed in New Guinea. See Barry Kent MacKay, '(A Little about) Fur and (a Lot about) Feathers: the Animal Cruelty No One Talks About ... or Remembers', at www.api4animals.org/doc.asp?ID=494.
5 After the phrase *regio psittacorum*, inscribed along the southern border of Gerardus Mercator's 1569 world chart (Schwartz, *The Culture of the Copy*, p. 148).
6 Charles Sturt, *Narrative of an Expedition into Central Australia* (London, 1849), vol. 1, pp. 63–4.
7 See Michel Butor, *Inventory: Essays*, ed. R. Howard (London, 1968), p. 210.

8 John Sparks with Tony Soper, *Parrots: A Natural History* (London, 1990), p. 204.

9 Oliver Goldsmith, quoted by Sir Thomas Dick Lauder and Capt. Thomas Brown, 'Intellectual and Imitative Faculties of Parrots', in *The Miscellany of Natural History* (Edinburgh, 1833), pp. 80–81.

10 Joseph M. Forshaw, *Parrots of the World* (Willoughby, NSW, 1989), p. 320.

11 Readers who don't know what this means, relax! 'Speaking without knowing is called "psittacism", but it is a practice not confined to parrots', quoted by www.funworks.com/library/p.htm.

12 Peter Steele, 'Dream Parrots', in *Invisible Riders* (North Ryde, NSW, 1999), p. 72.

13 See Tony Pittman, 'Prehistoric Cave Paintings Discovered', *Cage and Aviary Birds* (12 March 1994). Also www.bluemacaws.org/other2.htm.

14 Ovid, *The Erotic Poems*, trans. P. Green (Harmondsworth, 1982), p. 119.

15 Sparks with Soper, *Parrots,* p. 206.

16 Lewis Carroll, *The Annotated Alice*, notes by Martin Gardner (Harmondsworth, 1982), p. 272.

17 See the metamorphosis of the Roseate or Princess of Wales parakeet (pp. 127 and 130).

18 The skilled parrot psychologist advises that feather picking should not be rewarded. Toys that duplicate feathers should be offered instead. 'If the bird is snapping its feathers, dried pasta and ice cream sticks may be a likely substitute'. (Chris Davis, 'Some Basic Principles of Avian Behavior Modification', *Canadian Parrot Symposium* (1996), at www.silvio-co.com/cps/articles/1996/1996davis1.htm

1 PARROTICS

1 Joseph M. Forshaw, *Parrots of the World* (Willoughby, NSW, 1989), p. 19.
2 Ibid., p. 21.
3 Don Roberson, 'Parrots, Psittacidae', at www.montereybay.com/creagrus/parrots.html.
4 Ibid.
5 Ibid. See also 'Parrot', *Encyclopedia Britannica* (1911).
6 'Parrot', *Encyclopedia Britannica* (1911). See www.excite.co.jp/world/english/web/body/?wb_url=http%3A%2F%2Fencyclopedia.jrank.org%2FPAI_PAS%2FPARROT.
7 Ibid.
8 John Latham, *A General Synopsis of Birds* (London, 1776), p. 198.
9 Louise E. Robbins, *Elephant Slaves and Pampered Parrots: Exotic Animals in Eighteenth-century Paris* (Baltimore, MD, 2002), p. 19.
10 Ibid., p. 12.
11 George Edwards, *A Natural History of Birds* (London, 1751), p. 161.
12 Comte de Buffon, *Histoire naturelle des oiseaux* (Dordrecht, 1796), vol. VI, p. 115.
13 Errol Fuller, *Extinct Birds* (London, 1987), p. 131.
14 Anon., *Histoire des animaux* (Avignon, 1811), pp. 239-40.
15 Deborah Poole, *Vision, Race, and Modernity* (Princeton, NJ, 1997).
16 In John Sparks with Tony Soper, *Parrots: A Natural History* (London, 1990), p. 121.
17 Baldwin Spencer and F. J. Gillen, quoted in Emile Durkheim and Marcel Mauss, *Primitive Classification*, trans. R. Needham (London, 1963), p. 38.
18 Charles Mountford, *Nomads of the Australian Desert* (Sydney, 1976), p. 485 and pls 636, 637.
19 Ibid., p. 497.
20 John of Salisbury, *Policraticus*, in *Frivolities of Courtiers and Footprints of Philosophers*, trans. C. J. Nederman (Cambridge, 1990), p. 182.

21 Lucien Lévy-Bruhl, *How Natives Think*, trans. L. A. Clare (Princeton, NJ, 1985), p. 49.

22 Durkheim and Mauss, *Primitive Classification*, p. 6.

23 Martin Prechtel, *Long Life, Honey in the Heart: A Story of Initiation and Eloquence from the Shores of a Mayan Lake* (New York, 1999), p. 152.

24 Ibid., p. 153.

25 See www.exoticbird.com/online_parrots/intro001.html.

26 Sparks with Soper, *Parrots*, p. 102.

27 Jorge Luis Borges, 'El idioma analitico de John Wilkins', in *Otras inquisiciones* (Buenos Aires, 1960), p. 142, quoted by Christoph Kaderas in 'Why Sparrows and Dragons Belong to the Same Species: On the Taxonomic Method in Old Chinese Encyclopaedias', *Proceedings of the Fifth Conference of the International Society for the Study of European Ideas (ISSEI)*, 1996. At homepage.univie.ac.at/martin.potschka/ISSEI1996.htm.

28 Kaderas, 'Why Sparrows and Dragons Belong to the Same Species'.

29 Donald Levine, *The Flight from Ambiguity: Essays in Social and Cultural Theory* (Chicago, 1985), p. 8.

30 Craig Conley, 'From the Story of the Flood to Who Killed Laura Palmer: Documented Words that Talking Birds Never Said, Should Have Said, or Refused To Say', (1999), at www.blueray.com/wordsworth/literature/silent.html.

31 James L. Murphy, 'Breeding Parrots for human companionship: Genetic Selection for the Habitat of your Living Room', *Canadian Parrot Symposium* (1999), at www.silvio-co.com/cps/articles/1999/1999/jmurphy1.htm.

32 Rafael Alberti, *Selected Poems*, trans. B. Belitt (Berkeley, CA, 1966), p. 168.

33 Paul Willis, 'Dinosaurs and Birds, the Story' (1998), at www.abc.net.au/science/slab/dinobird/story.

34 Ernst Mayr, review of Alan Feduccia, *The Origin and Evolution of Birds* (New Haven, CT, 1996) at www.findarticles.com/p/articles/ mi_qa3746/is_199704/ai_n8765352.

35 Robert Sanders, 'Parrot Fossil from the Cretaceous Pushes Back Origin of Modern Land Birds' (1998), at www.berkeley.edu/news/berkeleyan/1998/1118/fossil.htm.

36 Although there is some question whether these Eocene bones are true progenitors. See www.masterliness.com/a/Psittaci formes.htm.

37 'Parrot', *Encyclopedia Britannica* (1911).

38 Ibid.

39 Forshaw, *Parrots of the World*, p. 20.

40 'Parrot', *Encyclopedia Britannica* (1911).

41 Sparks with Soper, *Parrots*, pp. 23–4.

42 Gerald Sider, 'When Parrots Learn To Talk, and Why They Can't: Domination, Deception, and Self-deception in Indian–White Relations', *Comparative Studies in Society and History*, XXIX (1987), p. 6.

43 Sparks with Soper, *Parrots*, p. 104.

44 'Parrot', *Encyclopedia Britannica* (1911), and *Oxford English Dictionary* (1989), XI, p. 253.

45 'Parrot', *Encyclopedia Britannica* (1911), and *Oxford English Dictionary* (1989), XI, p. 191.

46 *Oxford English Dictionary* (1989), XII, p. 37.

47 *Le Grand Robert de la langue française* (1973) entry for 'Jacquot', p. 94.

48 Boria Sax, *The Mythical Zoo: An Encyclopedia of Animals in World Myth, Legend and Literature* (Santa Barbara, CA, 2001), p. 187.

49 Phil Smith, 'Parrots in my Head', *The Listener* (19 April 1979).

50 Applied to fossilized parrot remains dated from the Lower Eocene (54–38 million years ago). See www.home.earthlink.net/~misaak/taxonomy/taxEtym.htm.

51 Jules Verne, *The Complete Twenty Thousand Leagues Under the Sea*, trans. E. J. Mickel (Bloomington, IN, 1991), p. 459.

52 See www.geocities.com/wcsscience/thegiant/squid.html.

53 See www.centralpets.com/animals/birds/parrots/prt1171.html.

54 Edward Conze, ed. and trans., *The Buddha's Law Among the Birds* (Oxford, 1974), p. 51.

55 'The Story of the Husband and the Parrot', *The Arabian Nights*. See www.chennaionline.com/children/parrot.asp.

56 *The Jataka; or, Stories of the Buddha's Former Births*, ed. E. B. Cowell, trans. from the Pali by W.H.D. Rouse (Cambridge, 1895), vol. II, no. 198. See www.pitt.edu/~dash/type0237.html.

57 M. Maurice Bloomfield, 'On Talking Birds in Hindu Fiction', *Festschrift Ernst Windish* (Leipzig, 1914), quoted by N. Rosenberg in 'An annotated collection of parrot jokes', dissertation, Indiana University, 1964, Folklore Archive, p. 3.

58 Marcus Boon, *The Road of Excess: A History of Writers on Drugs* (Cambridge, MA, 2002), p. 127.

59 Fahad Daftary, *The Assassin Legends* (London, 1994), p. 32.

60 Ibid., pp. 109–10.

61 John Lydgate, *The Minor Poems*, 2 vols (London, 1934), vol. II, no. 70, l. 89.

62 Pliny the Elder, *Natural History*, trans. H. Rackham (London, 1938–63) vol. X, p. 369.

63 T. H. White, *The Book of Beasts* (London, 1952), p. 113.

64 Aristotle, 'History of Animals', in *The Complete Works*, ed. J. Barnes, 2 vols (Princeton, NJ, 1984), vol. I, p. 934.

65 Ibid.

66 Vincent Hunink, 'An Apuleian Parrot' (on Apul. Fl. 12), *Acta Classica*, XLIII (2000), pp. 71–9, at www.let.kun.nl/V.Hunink/ documents/apu_parrot.htm.

67 See ref. 53 above.

68 Pliny the Elder, *Natural History*, Book X, LIX, p. 309.

69 See ref. 53 above.

70 Jean-Baptiste-Louis Gresset, 'Ver-Vert', at http://gallica.bnf.fr/ Fonds_Textes/T0088571.htm.

71 Gresset, 'Ver-Vert', ll. 105–7.

72 Julia Stewart in *The Independent* (25 April 2000), p. 9.

73 In Sir Thomas Dick Lauder and Capt. Thomas Brown, 'Intellectual and Imitative Faculties of Parrots', in *The Miscellany of Natural History* (Edinburgh, 1833), this association is preserved in the scientific names – 'The Amazon parrot (*Psittacus aestivus*)

and the Gray parrot (*Psittacus erythaeus*) are most susceptible of education' (p. 86). Nowadays *Psittacus* is the name of the African grey, its South American counterparts having the family name *Amazona*. Robert Hole, *Parrots of the World Checklist*. See www.interaktv.com/BIRDS/Psittlongver.html.

74 T. Percy Armstrong, 'Parrots in the Middle Ages', *Notes and Queries*, 169:20 (1935), 16 November, p. 353.

75 According to Von Humboldt, see White, *The Book of Beasts*, p. 113. See also Sue Farlow, 'Bearers of a Lost Language', ParrotChronicles.com (September–October 2002), where the vocal archaeologists are said to be Orange-winged and Blue-front Amazons.

76 Sir Thomas Dick Lauder tells the story ('Intellectual and Imitative Faculties of Parrots', pp. 56–7).

77 Ibid., p. 66.

78 Ibid., p. 67.

79 Bob Dylan, 'Farewell Angelina'. See www.dylanchords.com/34_ bootleg/farewell_angelina.htm.

80 Irene Pepperberg, 'Studies to Determine the Intelligence of African Grey Parrots', *Canadian Parrot Symposium*, 1994, at www.silvio-co.com/cps/articles/1994/1994pepperberg1.htm.

81 Barbara Katz, 'Mirror, mirror, on the wall'. See www.africangreys.com/articles/relationships/mirror.htm.

82 Diana L. May, 'Field studies of African grey parrots in the Central African Republic', *Proceedings of the International Aviculturists Society*, (January 1996), at www.funnyfarmexotics. com/IAS/greyfield.

83 Hugh Lofting, *The Voyages of Doctor Dolittle* (1922) at www.laits.utexas.edu/hebrew/personal/language/animals/doolittles.html.

84 Sarah Graham, 'Protecting St Vincent Amazon Parrots', *Scientific American* (4 September 2001). See www.sciam.com/article.cfm?articleID

85 Tony Juniper, *Spix's Macaw: The Race to Save the World's Rarest Bird* (New York, 2003).

86 'Parrot', *Encyclopedia Britannica*, (1911).
87 Tony Silva, *A Monograph of Endangered Parrots* (Pickering, Ontario, 1989), p. 156.
88 Ibid., p. 151.
89 Rainer Maria Rilke, 'The Parrot House [Papagaien-Park]', in *New Poems*, trans. S. Cohn (Manchester, 1992), pp.213–14.
90 Robbins, *Elephant Slaves and Pampered Parrots*, p. 279, note 37.
91 Lauder and Brown, 'Intellectual and Imitative Faculties of Parrots', pp. 69–70.
92 Gordon Brotherston, *Book of the Fourth World: Reading the Native Americas through their Literature* (New York, 1992), p. 60.
93 Craig Conley, 'Birdwatching Among the Ruins: Mexico's Mythical Macaws', www.blueray.com/wordsworth/mythology/mayan.html.
94 Vicky Unruh, *Latin American Vanguards: The Art of Contentious Encounters* (Berkeley, CA, 1994), p. 255.
95 Claude Levi-Strauss, *Tristes tropiques*, trans. J. and D. Weightman (London, 1973), p. 219.
96 Murphy, 'Breeding Parrots for Human Companionship', p. 2.
97 Robbins, *Elephant Slaves and Pampered Parrots*, p. 10.
98 Jules S.-C. Dumont D'Urville, *Two Voyages to the South Seas*, trans. H. Rosenman (Carlton, Victoria, 1988), vol. I, p. 141.
99 Chris Wallace-Crabbe, 'Puck Disembarks', in *For Crying Out Loud* (Oxford, 1990), p. 43.
100 Australian Museum, 2000 see www.lostkingdoms.com.facts/factsheet26.htm.
101 See www.exotictropicals.com/encyclo/birds/cockatoos.htm.
102 This and previous quotations are from Rosemary Dobson, 'Child with a Cockatoo', in *Child with a Cockatoo and Other Poems* (Sydney, 1955), pp. 18–19.
103 *Notes and Queries* (29 March 1930), p. 224.
104 John Morieson, 'The Night Sky of the Boorong, Partial Reconstruction of a Disappeared Culture in North-West Victoria', MA thesis, University of Melbourne, 1996, p. 113, asserts that 'This custom is still in use today'.

105   Lauder and Brown, 'Intellectual and Imitative Faculties of Parrots', p. 90.
106   Sir George Grey, *Expeditions in Western Australia, 1837–1839* (London, 1841), vol. II, p. 282.
107   See *Sunday Mail* (Queensland) (8 July 2003).
108   See www.exotictropicals.com/encyclo/birds/cockatoos/ CockatoosProfile.htm.
109   One answer is that it can bring about successful experiments in hybridization. The correct identification of likely 'surrogates' for the Spix macaw is vital if something of the Spix genome is to be preserved: a strange case of the word made flesh. (Donald Brightsmith, 'What Is in a Name? Avoiding the Chaos of Common Names', *Bird Talk Magazine* (May 1999). See www.duke.edu/~djb4/What%20is%20in%20a%20name%20Bird %20Talk.htm.).

2 PARROTERNALIA

1   Paul Bodington, 'Brisbane's Footy Tipping Cockatoo', at www.abc.net.au/brisbane/stories/s914893.htm.
2   At www.pabulletin.com/secure/data/vol32/32-1/18.html.
3   *Notes and Queries* (16 November 1935), p. 353.
4   Satya Prakash Chowdhary, 'Physics, Psychology and Astrology, Parrots, Hexagrams and Numbers Synchronicity: An A-causal Connecting Principle', at usrwww.mpx.com.au/skinbags/ id47.htm.
5   Munjul Ramanana, 'Parrot Trainer Fights To Keep 110-yr Tradition Alive', *Times of India* (21 September 2001).
6   Eugene Linden, *The Parrot's Lament: And Other True Tales of Animal Intrigue, Intelligence and Ingenuity* (London, 1999).
7   Heinrich Cornelius Agrippa, *Of Occult Philosophy, Book I (Part 2)*, digital edition by J. H. Peterson (2000), at www.esotericarchives.com/agrippa/agrippa1.htm.
8   Ibid.
9   C.E.O. Carter, 'The Sign Pisces', at www.digthatcrazyfarout.

com/carter/Carter_Pisces.htm.

10 James Arraj, 'The Mystery of Matter: Nonlocality, Morphic Resonance, Synchronicity and the Philosophy of Nature of St Thomas Aquinas' (1996), at www.innerexplorations.com/catchmeta/the.htm.

11 Ibid., chapter 8.

12 Quoted in Ben Davis, 'Ballet Mécanique', at www.mit.edu:8001/people/ davis/BalletMech.html.

13 Guillaume Apollinaire, 'Zone', at http//:media.ucsc.edu/classes/Thompson/Picasso.html

14 Bill Uzgalis, 'Paidea and Identity: Meditations on Hobbes and Locke', presented at the 20th World Congress of Philosophy in Boston (August 1998), at www.bu.edu/wcp/Papers/Mode/ ModeUzga.htm.

15 Quoted at www.languagehat.com/archives/001335.php, where the comments it has generated illustrate the parrot-like nature of the discourse these sites stimulate.

16 Hergé, *Red Rackham's Treasure* (London, 1960).

17 This and previous quotations from Martin Prechtel, *Long Life, Honey in the Heart: A Story of Initiation and Eloquence from the Shores of a Mayan Lake* (New York, 1999), pp. 153–9.

18 Ramanana, 'Parrot Trainer'. See www.gujaratplus.com/00-01archive/arc235.html

19 John Sparks, with Tony Soper, *Parrots: A Natural History* (London, 1990), p. 204.

20 Ibid., p. 204, and David Alderton, 'Talk the Squawk', *Guardian* (6 April 2002).

21 Ovid, *The Erotic Poems*, trans. Peter Green (Harmondsworth, 1986), p. 119.

22 Voltaire, 'The Black and the White', in *The Complete Romances of Voltaire* (New York, 1927); quoted by Craig Conley, www.blueray.com/wordsworth/literature/silent.html.

23 Boccaccio, *De genealogia deorum*, IV, xli, at www.oiseauxparleurs.org/site.php?page=historique&lang=fr, a good source of ancient and medieval parrot tales.

24 Lewis Carroll, *The Annotated Alice*, notes by Martin Gardner
    (Harmondsworth, 1982); quoted by Craig Conley at
    www.blueray.com/wordsworth/literature/silent.html.
25 Julian Barnes, *Flaubert's Parrot*, quoted by Craig Conley at
    www.blueray.com/wordsworth/literature/silent.html.
26 Sacheverell Sitwell, 'The Parrot' (1922) at
    www.theotherpages.org/poems/sitwell2.html.
27 Virginia Woolf, *Jacob's Room* (1922), chapter 9, at
    www.online-literature.com/virginia_woolf/jacob-room/9/.
28 *Notes and Queries*, 4th ser., I (25 January 1868), p. 86.
29 Ben Jonson, 'The Epicene', in *Selected Works*, ed. H. Levin
    (New York, p. 322.
30 Louise E. Robbins, *Elephant Slaves and Pampered Parrots: Exotic
    Animals in Eighteenth-century Paris* (Baltimore, MD, 2002), p. 24.
31 Hsueh T'ao, *Brocade River Poems: Selected Works of the Tang
    Dynasty Courtesan Xue Tao,* trans. J. Larsen (Princeton, NJ, 1987,
    p. 98; and p. 54 for poem.
32 Informally extracted from Robbins, *Elephant Slaves and
    Pampered Parrots*, pp. 142–53.
33 Jonathan Swift, 'Cadenus and Vanessa', in *Poetical Works*, ed.
    H. Davis (Oxford, 1967), p. 115.
34 William Wordsworth, *Poetical Works*, ed. T. Hutchinson
    (Oxford, 1969): 'The Contrast. The Parrot and the Wren', p. 130.
35 Catherine Ingrassia, 'Texts, Lies and the Marketplace . . .', at
    www.has.vcu.edu/eng/symp/ing_txt.htm.
36 Joyce Dyer, 'A Green and Yellow Parrot', in *The Awakening: A Novel
    of Beginnings* (New York, 1993), pp. 35–6.
37 Annamarie Jagose, 'Hollywood Lesbians', *Genders*, XXXII (2000),
    p. 25. See www.genders.org/g32/g32_jagose.html.
38 Mary E. Papke, 'What Do Women Want?', at
    www.centerforbookculture.org/context.no11/Papke.html.
39 At www.exoticbird.com/online_parrots/intro001.html.
40 Ovid, *Erotic Poems*, p. 118.
41 Ibid., p. 119.
42 J. M. Forshaw, *Parrots of the World* (Willoughby, NSW, 1989),

pp. 35–6.

43 *Gentleman's Magazine*, XVIII (October 1748), p. 440.

44 See www.hevanet.com/alexwest/parrots/symbolist.html and www.sexuality.org/l/polyamar/polyfaq.html.

45 *Kama Sutra of Vatsyayana*, trans. R. Burton and F. F. Arbuthnot (Atlantic Highlands, NJ, 1982), p. 74.

46 Ibid., p. 133.

47 Tony Silva in *A Monograph of Endangered Parrots* (Pickering, Ontario, 1989), p. 139, for this and previous quotation.

48 James R. Kincaid, *My Secret Life: An Erotic Diary of Victorian London*, at www.my-secret-life.info/

49 Arnaut de Carcassés, *Tale of the Parrot (Novas del papagai)*, trans. R. G. Arthur (Cambridge, Ontario, 1999), ll. 137–40, at onlinebooks.library.upenn.edu/webbin/book/browse?type=title&index=20623&key=tale%20of%20the%20pa

50 Quoted in D. Ades, 'The Transcendental Surrealism . . . of Joseph Cornell', in *Joseph Cornell*, exh. cat. (New York, 1980), p. 37, at www.guggenheimcollection.org/site/artist_work_md_32_1.html.

51 Edward Quinn, *Max Ernst* (London), p. 28.

52 Ibid., quoting Patrick Waldberg.

53 Edith Sitwell, 'Come the Great Popinjay', in *Collected Poems* (London, 1957), p. 126.

54 *Blackwood's Magazine* (March 1848), p. 96.

55 *Blackwood's Magazine* (July 1849), p. 96.

56 Michel de Montaigne, 'Of the Education of Children', at www.historyguide.org/intellect/montaigne.html.

57 Anne-Marie Bowery, 'Responding to Socrates' Pedagogical Provocation', at www.bu(?).edu/wcp/Papers/Anci/AnciBowe.htm.

58 Neil V. Rosenberg, 'An Annotated Collection of Parrot Jokes', dissertation, Indiana University, 1964, Folklore Archive, pp. 26–60.

59 James George Frazer, *Balder the Beautiful* (London, 1876), vol. II, pp. 97–8.

60 Ibid., p. 98.

61 James George Frazer, *Spirits of the Corn and the Wild*, 2 vols (London, 1912), vol. I, p. ix

62 Rosenberg, 'An Annotated Collection of Parrot Jokes', p. 4.

63 'The Story of the Husband and the Parrot', at www.chennaionline.com/children/parrot.asp.

64 'The Parrot Shah', at www.e-text.org/text/Grimms%20Fairy %20/Tales%20-%20Parrot%20Shah.txt.

65 Joseph Conrad, *Under Western Eyes* (London, 1925), p. 3.

66 Erich Jarvis, 'The Science Show', Radio National (22 March 2003), at www.abc.net.au/rn/science/ss/stories/S800735.htm.

67 James Murphy, 'Breeding Parrots for Human Companionship: Genetic Selection for the Habitat of your Living Room', *Canadian Parrot Symposium* (1999), at www.silvio-co.com/cps/articles/1999/1999/jmurphy1.htm.

68 Sally Blanchard, 'Basic Principles of Psittacine Behavior: How They Apply to Companion Parrots', *Canadian Parrot Symposium* (1999), at www.silvio-co.com/cps/articles/1999/1999blanchard1.htm

69 Chris Davis, 'Understanding Companion Bird Behavior: A New Paradigm Behavior Modification To Enhance the Human/Pet Parrot Relationship', *Canadian Parrot Symposium* (1998), at www.silvio-co.com/cps/articles/1998/1998davis1.htm.

70 Carroll, *The Annotated Alice*, p. 272.

71 *The Age* (5 September 2003), p. 11.

72 Chris Biro, 'Why I Think Birds Should Be Allowed to Fly', at www.parrotchronicles.com, May–June 2003, issue 11.

73 Murphy, 'Breeding parrots for Human Companionship'.

74 Rosenberg, 'An Annotated Collection of Parrot Jokes', pp. 49–50.

75 Steve Martin, 'Behavior', at www.parrotchronicles.com/depart ments/lookoflove_behavior.htm.

76 Dr C. G. Boeree, 'Psychotherapy', at www.ship.edu/~cgboeree/psychotherapy.html.

77 Ibid.

78 Ibid.

79 Linden, *The Parrot's Lament*, pp. 41–2.

80 Vadim Linetski, 'The Natural Beauty of Deconstruction', at

www.pd.org/topos/perforations/perf10/natbeauty.html.

81 A non-parrotic economy of reproduction means that readers need to locate this at Gary Larsen, *The Far Side Desk Calendar* (1997), week March 17–23.

82 George Rason, 'Aviary Design', at www.silvio-co.com/cps/articles/1995/1995rason1.htm.

83 From www.animalstop.com/animalstoppages/Whatsizecageis bestformybird.html.

84 See www.hectorsprettybirds.homestead.com/toysandcages. html.

85 Rason, 'Aviary Design'.

86 John Skelton, 'Speke Parott', in *The Complete English Poems*, ed. J. Scattergood (Harmonsworth, 1983), l. 70.

87 For this discussion, see Linetski, 'The Natural Beauty of Deconstruction', quoting Elizabeth Gaskell, *Cranford* (Harmondsworth, 1978), p. 338.

88 See Timothy Matthews, *Reading Apollinaire: Theories of Poetic Language* (Oxford, 1987), p. 146 (my translation).

89 At www.abc.net.au/science/news/archive/EnviroRepublish _453637.htm. The reference is to Kathryn E. Arnold, Ian P. F. Owens and N. Justin Marshall, 'Fluorescent signalling in parrots', *Science*, 92(4 January 2002).

90 John Shaw Neilson, *Selected Poems* (Sydney, 1980).

91 John A. Hodgson, 'An Other Voice: Ventriloquism in the Romantic Period', at users.ox.ac.uk/~scato385/hodgson.htm.

92 'Terry Bennett and Joy', www.chicagotelevision.com/ bennett.htm.

93 Hodgson, 'An Other Voice'.

94 Wallace Stevens, 'The Comedian as the Letter C', in *Collected Poems* (London, 1966), p. 32.

95 Vicky Unruh, *Latin American Vanguards*, p. 208.

96 Ibid., p. 215.

97 For this and previous quotations, ibid., pp. 252–8.

98 Gerald Sider, 'When Parrots Learn To Talk, and Why They Can't: Domination, Deception and Self-Deception in

Indian–White Relations', *Comparative Studies in Society and History*, XXIX (1987), p. 7.

99 Paul Carter, *The Lie of the Land* (London, 1996), pp. 188–9.

100 Sir Thomas Dick Lauder and Capt. Thomas Brown, 'Intellectual and Imitative Faculties of Parrots', in *The Miscellany of Natural History* (Edinburgh, 1833), p. 63.

101 'Colonel O'Kelly's Parrot', *Notes and Queries*, 3rd ser., VIII/199 (21 October 1865), p. 335.

102 Ibid.

103 Robbins, *Elephant Slaves and Pampered Parrots*, p. 11.

104 T. H. White, *The Book of Beasts* (London, 1952).

105 At www.studyflight.ru/humour.shtml.

106 Pauline Melville, 'The Parrot and Descartes', in *The Migration of Ghosts* (London, 2000), quoted at www.infoplease.com/idea/ AO778013.html.

107 Pamela Clark, 'The Social Climate', pp. 1–7, 5, at www.parrot-steward.com/pages/readingroom4.ht.

108 Ibid., p. 6.

109 Ma Shouzhen, 'The Parrot', in *Women Writers of Traditional China*, ed. Kang-I San Chang and Hann Saussy (Stanford, 1997), p. 231.

110 Herbert Mason, *A Legend of Alexander; and The Merchant and the Parrot* (Notre Dame, IN, 1986), p. 70.

111 Gabriel García Márquez, *Love in the Time of Cholera* (New York, 1990). See Craig Conley at www.blueray.com/wordsworth/ literature/silent.html.

112 Ma Shouzhen, 'The Parrot', p. 231.

113 Italo Calvino, 'Introduction', in *Italian Folktales*, trans. G. Martin (New York, 1980), p. xxxi.

114 Francisco Maldonado de Guevara, *El Primer Contacto de Blancos y Gentes de Color en América* (Valladolid, 1924), p. 47.

115 Charles Sturt, *Narrative of an Expedition into Central Australia* (London, 1849), I, p. 64.

116 Michel Serres, 'Laughs: The Misappropriated Jewels, or a Close Shave for the Prima Donna', *Art & Text*, IX (Autumn 1983), p. 17.

Iago in the English translation, the macaw's name in Hergé's
original is 'Co-co'.

117 David M. Levine, 'A Festival of Parrots', *Antioch Review*, XLVI/1
(1988), p. 52.

118 Ibid., p. 53.

119 Linden, *The Parrot's Lament*, p. 41.

120 *Herald Sun* (Melbourne, Australia) (24 February 2004), p. 24.

121 Maria Cristina Paganoni, 'Doubles, Dreams and Death in *Little
Dorrit*', *Culture. Annali dell'Istituto di Lingue della Facoltà di Scienze
Politiche*, no. 14 (2000), at users.unimi.it/dickens/essays.html.

122 Martial, *Epigrams*, trans. D. R. Shackleton Bailey, 3 vols,
(Cambridge, MA, 1993), vol. III, pp. 254–5.

123 Dan Gunn, 'Pieces of Eight! Coquilles Saint-Jacques! Of parrots,
Parents and Prostheses', Tekhnema 3/'A Touch of Memory'/
Spring 1996, at http://tekhnema.free.fr/3Gunn.htm.

124 Ono Komachi, *Poems, Stories, No Plays* (New York, 1993), p. 67.

125 This and previous quotations from John Skelton, 'Speke Parott',
pp. 231–6. See also notes on pp. 454–5.

3 PARROTOLOGY

1 Tony Silva, *A Monograph of Endangered Parrots* (Pickering, Ontario,
1989), pp. 293–4.

2 Quoted by Louise E. Robbins, *Elephant Slaves and Pampered
Parrots: Exotic Animals in Eighteenth-century Paris* (Baltimore, MD
2002), p. 25.

3 Ibid., p. 240, note 2.

4 Noel Snyder, *The Carolina Parakeet: Glimpses of a Vanished Bird*
(Princeton, NJ, 2004), p. 138.

5 Gerardo Reichel-Dolmatoff, 'Cosmology as Ecological Analysis:
A view from the Rain Forest', *Man, Journal of the Royal Anthro-
pological Institute*, XI/3 (1977), p. 308.

6 At www.loroparque-fundacion.org/Objectives.

7 At www.chycor.co.uk/paradise-park/world.htm.

8 At www.worldtwitch.com/thick-billed_parrot.htm.

9 At www.africanconservation.org/southafrics3.html.

10 At www.rareconservation.org, and Rosemary Low, 'Parrot
    Conservation Education: The Way Forward', at
    www.funnyfarmexotics.com/IAS/schedule2003.htm.

11 W. R. Kingston, quoted by Silva in *A Monograph of Endangered
    Parrots*, p. 190.

12 Tony Juniper, *Spix's Macaw: The Race to Save the World's Rarest
    Bird* (New York, 2003).

13 This and previous quotation from Barry Kent MacKay in '(A Little
    about) Fur and (a lot about) Feathers: The Animal Cruelty No
    One Talks About . . . or Remembers', at http://www.api4animals.
    org/doc.asp?ID=494.

14 Alan Boyle, MSNBC News, at http://www.msnbc.com/news/
    575282.asp?cp1=1.

15 Silva, *A Monograph of Endangered Parrots*, p. 166.

16 This and previous quotations from Irene M. Pepperberg,
    'Studies to Determine the Intelligence of African Grey Parrots',
    at www.silvio-co.com/cps/articles/1994/1994pepperberg1.htm.

17 Barbara Katz, 'Mirror, Mirror on the Wall', at www.african-
    greys.com/articles/relationships/mirror.htm.

18 Lauren Julius Harris, 'Footedness in Parrots: Three Centuries of
    Research, Theory, and Mere Surmise', *Canadian Journal of
    Psychology*, XLIII/3 (1989), p. 374.

19 *Notes and Queries*, 4th ser., III/76 (12 June 1869), p. 554.

20 In Harris, 'Footedness in Parrots', p. 375.

21 Ibid., p. 376.

22 Ibid., p. 377.

23 Ibid., p. 371

24 Ibid., p. 389.

25 Ibid., p. 391.

26 Anon., *Histoire des animaux* (Avignon, 1811), p. 240.

27 Errol Fuller, *Extinct Birds* (London, 1987), for example plate XXIX
    of the Black-fronted parakeet and the Society parakeet.

28 Walter Rothschild, *Extinct and Vanishing Birds of the World*

(London, 1909), and see also Fuller, *Extinct Birds*, pp. 130–31.

29 Fuller, *Extinct Birds*, p. 135.

30 *The Age* (29 April 2003).

31 Fuller, *Extinct Birds*, p. 136.

32 Sidney Nolan, diary notes 31 August 1949, in Jinx-Nolan Papers, quoted in *Sidney Nolan: Desert and Drought Environment*, exh. cat., at the National Gallery of Victoria (2003).

33 Dorothy Porter, 'The Night Parrot', in *The Night Parrot* (Wentworth Falls, NSW, 1984), p. 17.

34 'Of Gentility Mongering', *Blackwood's Edinburgh Magazine*, LIII/329 (March 1843), p. 379.

35 John James Audubon, *Birds of America*, IV, at www.audubon.org/bird/BoA/F28_G1a.htm.

36 Joseph M. Forshaw, 'The Changing Face of Aviculture in Australia: Comments from a "Professional Critic"', *Canadian Parrot Symposium* (1998), at www.silvio-co.com/cps/articles/1998/1998forshaw1.htm.

37 Peter Steele, 'Dream Parrots', in *Invisible Riders* (North Ryde, NSW, 1999), p. 72.

38 Joseph Roach, *Cities of the Dead: Circum-Atlantic Performance* (New York, 1996), p. 130.

39 Ibid., pp. 130–31.

40 Eugene Linden, *The Parrot's Lament; and Other True Tales of Animal Intrigue, Intelligence and Ingenuity* (London, 1999), p. 42.

Bibliography

Alderton, David, *Parrots* (London, 1992)

Beissinger, S. R., 'Ecological Mechanisms of Extinction', *Proceedings of the National Academy of Sciences of the United States of America*, XCVII/22 (24 October 2000), pp. 11688–9

Beissinger, S. R., and N.F.R. Snyder, eds, *New World Parrots in Crisis* (Washington, DC, 1992)

Boehrer, Bruce Thomas, *Parrot Culture* (Philadelphia, 2004)

Brightsmith, Donald J., 'Competition, Predation and Nest Niche Shifts among Tropical Cavity Nesters: Phylogeny and Natural History Evolution of Parrots (Psittaciformes) and Trogons (Trogoniformes)', *Journal of Avian Biology*, XXXVI (2005), pp. 64–73

Collar, N. J., 'Family Psittacidae (Parrots)', in *Handbook of the Birds of the World*, ed. J. del Hoyo, et al. (Barcelona, 1992–2003)

Forshaw, Joseph M., and William T. Cooper, *Parrots of the World*, 3rd edn (Melbourne, 2002)

Fuller, Errol, *Extinct Birds* (London, 1987)

Hyde, Graeme, ed., *Australian Aviculture* (Melbourne, 1983)

Juniper, Tony, *Spix's Macaw* (London, 2003)

Juniper, Tony, and Mike Parr, *Parrots: A Guide to Parrots of the World* (New Haven, CT, 1997)

Lambourne, Maureen, *The Art of Bird Illustration* (Royston, 2001)

Low, Rosemary, *Endangered Parrots* (London, 1984)

Pepperberg, Irene, *The Alex Studies: Cognitive and Communicative Abilities of Grey Parrots* (Cambridge, MA, 1999)

Robbins, Louise E., *Elephant Slaves and Pampered Parrots: Exotic*

Animals in Eighteenth-Century Paris (Baltimore, MD, 2002)

Schwartz, Hillel, *The Culture of the Copy: Striking Likenesses, Unreasonable Facsimiles* (New York, 1996)

Silva, Tony, *A Monograph of Endangered Parrots* (Pickering, Ontario, 1989)

Snyder, Noel F. R., *The Carolina Parakeet: Glimpses of a Vanished Bird* (Princeton, NJ, 2004)

Sparks, John, with Tony Soper, *Parrots: A Natural History* (London, 1990)

Strunden, Hans, *Papageien einst und jetzt* (Bomlitz, 1984)

Associations and Websites

CANADIAN PARROT SYMPOSIUM (www.silvio-co.com/cps/),
    'an international convention for those interested in keeping or
    breeding parrots', has articles about parrot (and parrot owner)
    behaviour.

COMPANION PARROT (www.companionparrot.com) describes itself as
    'the thinking person's parrot magazine', and is
    produced by the Parrot Behavioral Information Council.

CONVENTION ON INTERNATIONAL TRADE IN ENDANGERED SPECIES
    (CITES) can be read in full at www.cites.org/.

LINKS at www.thewildconnection.org/ let you 'fly around the world
    with us to some of the best conservation, education, and parrot
    sites on the entire web'.

LORO PARQUE FUNDACION has a hybrid mission, aiming
    'to improve the conservation status of threatened parrots and
    their natural habitats and to encourage 'responsible breeding'
    (Information at www.loroparque-fundacion.org/).

PARROT CHRONICLES (www.parrotchronicles.com) describes itself as
    'your number-one source of health, behaviour and care advice for
    companion parrots'.

PARROT LINE UK (www.parrotline.org/) is 'the largest parrot rescue charity in the United Kingdom'.

PARROT LINK (www.parrot-link.co.uk) is 'the original UK web site and breeders' directory for parrots, macaws, parrakeets and all parrot-like species, their owners and friends'.

PARROT PAGES (www.parrotpages.com) provides links to associations variously devoted to parrot research, preservation, conservation and aviculture.

PARROT SOCIETY UK has a website (www.parrotsocietyuk/org/) designed to 'encourage . . . keeping, breeding, husbandry, research and conservation'. Note that many parrot species have their own conservation societies. For details, simply google by species name and 'parrot conservation'.

RARE CENTER (www.rareconservation.org/) supports the efforts of conservationists around the world 'to save magnificent natural landscapes and irreplaceable wildlife'.

RESEARCH CENTRE FOR AFRICAN PARROT CONSERVATION (www.african-conservation.org/) carries valuable reports on its current conservation initiatives.

THE ALEX FOUNDATION (www.alexfoundation.org/) describes Dr Irene Pepperberg's research into the cognitive and communicative abilities of greys and how you can help.

WORLD PARROT TRUST (www.worldparrottrust.org/) is a 'charity funding projects and promoting excellence in parrot conservation and welfare'.

Acknowledgements

Say 'parrot' and most friends I had found a story to tell. Thank you to all, and particular thanks to: Gannit Ankori, Gregory Burgess, Steve Connor, Teresa Crowley, Harry Gilonis, Peter King, Michael Leaman, Andrew McLennan, Beate Schaefer, Horst Trossbach, Leon van Schaik, Chris Wallace-Crabbe and John Wolseley.

David Derr, Patricia Golden, Noel Hart, Tony Pittman, Sue Rees and Beate Schaefer most generously contributed their work to the enterprise. I must also thank the librarians of the Zoological Society of London for their time and help with picture research.

Two books have a special place in my research aviary: Hillel Schwartz's brilliant *The Culture of the Copy* and Elaine Robbins's no less wonderful *Elephant Slaves and Pampered Parrots*. The first gives the best, and certainly most succinct, account of parrot as mimic. The second is an East Indies of anecdotes illustrating the growth of our post-renaissance parrot dependence. Hillel Schwartz also most generously shared with me his bibliography of parrot references.

Publication of *Parrot* was assisted by grants from The Australian Academy of the Humanities, and the Faculty of Architecture, Building and Planning, University of Melbourne, with an additional publication grant from the University of Melbourne.

Photo Acknowledgements

The author and publishers wish to express their thanks to the below sources of illustrative material and/or permission to reproduce it. Some sources uncredited in the captions for reasons of brevity are also given below. We have not always been able to trace the copyright holders of all material, and where these efforts have not been successful, we would appreciate it if copyright holders would contact the publishers.

© ADAGP, Paris and DACS, London 2005: p. 36; Alte Pinakothek, Munich p. 56; Art Gallery of New South Wales, Sydney: p. 169; courtesy of the artists: pp. 82 (Beate Schaefer), 133 (David Derr), 171 (Noel Hart); photo Artothek p. 56; collection of the author: p.91; Biblioteca Estense, Modena: p. 58; Bibliothèque du Palais Bourbon, Paris: p. 75; British Library, London (MSOr.2626, fols. 7b-8a): p. 47; photo Jeff Carter: p. 11; © The Joseph and Robert Cornell Memorial Foundation/VAGA, New York/DACS, London 2005: p. 98; photo Bruno David: p. 63 (top); Doboistván Muzeum, Eger: p. 173; photo Patricia Golden: p. 98; from John Gould, *The Birds of Australia* (1840–48): p. 51; Graphisches Sammlung Albertina, Vienna: p. 62; Groeningemuseum, Bruges: p. 48; photos Cyril Laubscher: pp. 109, 130; Museo Lázaro Galdiano, Madrid: p. 52; photo Library of Congress, Washington, DC (Prints and Photographs Division): pp. 14 (British Cartoon Collection; LC-USZC4-6449), 105 (LC-G613-T-62779); Liverpool Museum: p. 136; photo Jean-Paul Lozouet: p. 33; photo Matthew Chase Ltd: p. 34; Metropolitan Museum of Art, New York: pp. 86 (H. O. Havemeyer Collection, Bequest of Mrs. H. O. Havemeyer, photo © 1979 The

Museum of Art), 95 (gift of Erwin Davis, photo © 1993 The Metropolitan Museum of Art); Musée de Versailles: p. 79; Musée des Beaux-Arts, Grenoble: p. 122; National Gallery of Australia, Canberra: p. 13 (gift of the Philip Morris Arts Grant); National Library of Australia, Canberra: pp. 11, 138, 146 (from John Hunter, *Birds and Flowers of New South Wales*, Rex Nan Kivell Collection, NK2039), 148, 167 (W. T. Cooper Collection); National Museum of the American Indian (Smithsonian Institution), Washington, DC: p. 60; The Natural History Museum, London: pp. 21, 24, 155, 162, 163, 177; Naturhistorisches Museum, Vienna: pp. 15, 139 (photo: author); photo Graeme Parker/*Herald Sun* (Australia) p. 96; photo Tony Pittman: p. 16; photo Susan Rees (sponsored by a Senior Fulbright Research Scholarship) p. 46; photos Rex Features: pp. 6 (Rex Features/Shane Partridge, 374497B), 9 (Rex Features/Eva Magazine, 252655B), 32 (145270C), 68 (197726A), 99 (Rex Features/Tim Rooke, 199388A) p. 129 (419849BH); Rijksmuseum, Amsterdam: p. 119; photos Rex Features/ Roger-Viollet: pp. 17 (© Collection Roger-Viollet, RV-383300), 52 (© Collection Roger-Viollet, RVB-12448), 55 (© Collection Roger-Viollet, RV-453327), 78 (© Collection Roger-Viollet, RV-389574), 79 (© Collection Roger-Viollet, RVB-06200), 100 (© B. Martinez/Collection Roger-Viollet; BM-74-6), 111 (© B. Martinez/Collection Roger-Viollet; RVB-13137), 125 (© Valsecchi/Alinari/Collection Roger-Viollet; ALI-VGA-F-000461-0000), 128 (ND/Collection Roger-Viollet; ND-2595A), 173 (Collection Roger-Viollet, RVB-04285); Römisch-Germanisches Museum, Köln: p. 39; Sammlung Frieder Burda, Baden-Baden: p. 158; State Library of New South Wales, Sydney: pp. 90, 165; State Library of Victoria, Melbourne: pp. 156, 161; Topkapi Saray Museum, Istanbul: p. 114, 178 (foot); Barbara Tucker: p. 41; University of Melbourne (Baillieu Library): pp. 116, 121; Victoria and Albert Museum, London, photos © V&A Picture Library: pp. 76 (CT35155), 103 (CT67322) 170 (CT67322); Wadsworth Atheneum Museum of Art, Hartford, CT: p. 143 (The Ella Gallup Sumner and Mary Catlin Sumner Collection Fund); Wardaman Aboriginal Corporation: p. 63 (top); photo Ron Daniel / World of Stock p. 57 (top); photos © Zoological Society of London: pp. 26 top, and foot (from George Edwards, *A Natural History of Birds*, 1751), 27 top (from the Comte de Buffon, *Histoire naturelle des oiseaux*, 1796), and foot, 53 (from S. Manetti, L. Lorenzi, V. Vanni, *Storia naturale degli Uccelli*, 1767), p. 57 (foot), 63, 102, 113, 127 (from Edward Lear, *Illustrations of the Family of Psittacidae, or Parrots*, 1832), 141 (from J. J. Audubon, *The Birds of America*, 1827–38), 159 (from George Edwards, *A Natural History of Birds*, 1751).

Index